EARLY OREGON DAYS

EARLY OREGON DAYS

By

Edwin D. Culp

The Caxton Printers, Ltd.
Caldwell, Idaho
1997

First Printing December 1987
Second Printing June 1997

Library of Congress Cataloging Publication Data

Culp, Edwin D.
    Early Oregon days.

    1. Railroads — Oregon — History. 2. Transportation —
Oregon — History. 3. Railroads — West (U.S.) — History.
4. Transportation — West (U.S.) — History. I. Title.
TF24.07C85   1986   385′.09795   86-23294
    ISBN 0-87004-314-5

Lithographed and bound in the United States of America by
The Caxton Printers, Ltd., Caldwell, Idaho 83605
161842

CONTENTS

FOREWORD

THE CAVALCADE OF Oregon history reads like a fascinating novel. In the beginning getting to Oregon meant walking, or by horseback or journeying across the seas by sailing vessel; the sailing vessel giving way to the steamboat and the covered wagon bringing families and their belongings. The steam engine running on iron rails opened up another era to be followed by the automobile and the jet airplane. One might ask what we can expect next?

Our early history was told by a variety of early writers. Foremost was Frances Fuller Victor's *River of the West* and *All Over Oregon and Washington*, both written in the 1870s. She entered the A. L. Bancroft historical enterprise at San Francisco in 1870 and turned out many volumes on Oregon history written from her vast accumulation of historical data. Francis Parkman in *Oregon Trail* contributed to the record of westward overland expansion while Richard Henry Dana describes beautifully the journey by sea in *Two Years Before the Mast*. Washington Irving notes the exploits of reaching Oregon by water and overland in his *Astoria*. Eva Emery Dye arrived in Oregon City after Dr. John McLoughlin, the father of Oregon, had died, but from friends and acquaintances, she was able to write *McLoughlin and Old Oregon* and followed this by *The Conquest — The True Story of Lewis and Clark*. Many have contributed to the history of the great state of Oregon.

When we look at the American West today, the focal point of the greatest human migration in the history of the world, it is somewhat difficult to realize only a few years ago Daniel Webster is said to have addressed the United States Senate in opposition to the idea of building a railroad to the Pacific Coast. He thought that savages and wild beasts along with high mountain ranges presented too big a problem. It is not altogether surprising that a statesman with the eminence of Daniel Webster should have held this view.

The Pacific Monthly, published in 1898 in Portland, was an excellent magazine covering scenery and stories of Oregon and the West. *Sunset Magazine*, founded the same year by the Southern Pacific Railroad using almost the same format and size, was edited to encourage rail traffic to see the entire Pacific Coast area. The railroad secured ownership of *The Pacific Monthly* and consolidated it with its own *Sunset Magazine*. This publication developed into a very successful advertising medium. In addition, the railroads using the *Sunset Magazine* printing and editorial staff prepared thousands of attractive booklets describing and illustrating the many towns and cities along their lines. The Southern Pacific covered the area from Portland to Ashland and included many short line branches while the Union Pacific did the same along its line bordering the south bank of the Columbia River and extending to the Idaho border. (During the first years of the century the SP and UP were a jointly operated rail line.)

Under the Land Grant Act the railroads

at the time of their construction were given lands by both the federal and state governments for development and colonization. The promotion work done by the "Advertising the West" program resulted in the vast wilderness of the Oregon country and the West becoming a great civilized community.

ACKNOWLEDGMENTS

THE LARGE MAJORITY of the photos used in this book were ones I acquired during my forty years in public relations work for one of the large railroads. In traveling over the state I met hundreds of people whose parents came to this state via the covered wagon. They were as proud of their Oregon ancestry as I am of mine. Many had early photographs and camera snapshots and they allowed me to have copies made and retain a print for myself. I am deeply indebted to the two commercial photographers, Charles Raymon Lindsay and our son, Curtis Edward Culp, who copied these pictures for me. My fussy demands of having a perfect picture must have tried their patience but I never heard a complaint.

My wife, Florence Watt Culp, proofread and double checked all of the written material in addition to keeping my thinking going in a straight direction. Our daughter, Gail Ruth Culp (Ryder) and my brother, Richard Dean Culp, from time to time would pat me on the back when I got to feeling sorry for myself about being overworked.

George Kraus and George Skorney, both public relations directors for the two largest railroads in this state, gave of their time with helpful suggestions as well as furnishing me with railroad photos. Those wonderful people at the state library and the city library here in Salem have the patience of Job in helping me locate information and gather statistics. Over the years members of the RAILROAD AND LOCOMOTIVE HISTORICAL SOCIETY and the NATIONAL RAILWAY HISTORICAL SOCIETY have loaned me photos from their private collections. I am ashamed to say but I have forgotten many of their names. Without this help I could never have accumulated this vast number of pictures.

EARLY OREGON DAYS

OREGON TIMETABLES

ROBERT GRAY — He came for furs and found an empire. On May 11, 1792 Captain Robert Gray from Boston nosed his eighty-three-foot fur trading schooner, *The Columbia Redivia*, through a dangerous line of breakers crossing the bar into the previously undiscovered Columbia River. Of all the dates in the history of the Oregon country none is more important from an American viewpoint than this one.

For his daring seamanship and good fortune, Gray was able to lay claim for the United States to a vast empire drained by the great river of the West. Gray, a thirty-six-year-old Yankee trader, came primarily for prized sea otter pelts. The Boston owners of the vessel had commissioned him to gather these from the natives to be sold in China; these profits to be turned into tea and brought back to Boston for more profits.

Captain Robert Gray

Capt. Gray named the river he discovered after his ship, the *Columbia*.

SCHEDULE:

Inbound: On May 11, 1792 Captain Gray made port and anchored at the mouth of the Columbia River. During the next few days he explored some fifteen miles of the great river.

Outbound: On May 20, 1792 after taking aboard fresh water in their casks and fresh salmon in the galley, Captain Gray again sailed out into the Pacific Ocean.

COLUMBIA in DESTRESS.
In Latitude 16.11 South Long.t 57.9 West December 11 1790

A drawing of the *Columbia* made by George Davidson, a crew member under Captain Robert Gray

Capt. Meriwether Lewis (1774–1809)
In command of the Lewis and Clark Expedition
which penetrated to the Columbia River.

Capt. William Clark (1770–1838)
One of the leaders of the famous Lewis and Clark
Expedition.

The Lewis and Clark Expedition
to Oregon

On May 14, 1804 a forty-five member party of American explorers set out from St. Louis, Missouri in search of a river route to the Pacific Ocean some two thousand uncharted miles to the west.

Over the course of the following eighteen months the party, which came to be called the Lewis and Clark Expedition after its leaders, explored and discovered a route that reached the Pacific and etched their names in the annals of history.

The idea of such an expedition was conceived by the nation's third president, Thomas Jefferson. Jefferson had acquired the vast Louisiana Purchase territory before the explorers set out. He wanted them to bring back information about its Indian tribes, plant and animal life, topography and geography, and trade potential.

SCHEDULE:

Westbound: Lewis and Clark and their men left St. Louis, Missouri, May, 1804. They passed The Dalles, Oregon, October 22, 1805 en route to the ocean. They reached the Pacific Ocean, November, 1805.

Eastbound: They started homeward bound, March 23, 1806. They reached St. Louis, September 23, 1806. The trip consumed two years, four months and nine days.

Although there was no anticipation of a holiday feast and none of the usual associations of Christmas, the ragged soldiers kept the holiday faith. William Clark, making his daily entry, wrote: "At daylight this morning we were awakened by the discharge of the firearms of all our party and a salute, shouts, and a song which the whole party joined in under our windows, after which they retired to their rooms and were cheerful all the morning."

Whatever the reason, after the salute, the shouts and the song, the day passed quietly. Clark, remembering no doubt the feasting and cheers of former Christmas', concluded

Christmas morning at Fort Clatsop in 1805

his entry for December 25, 1805: "We would have spent this day, the nativity of Christ, in feasting had we anything either to raise our spirits or even gratify our appetites. Our dinner consisted of elk, so much spoiled that we ate it through necessity, with some spoiled pounded fish and a few roots."

According to William Clark's diary, the group first sighted Celilo on October 22, 1805. The large mural in the Oregon State Capitol rotunda *(see opposite page)* shows Meriwether Lewis and William Clark *(center of scene)* and Sacajawea — "The Birdwoman," *(right)* who made the long trek with the expedition into the Oregon Country and the Pacific. In the background can be seen the beautiful Celilo Falls once called "Tumwater" or "Great Chute" by early travelers. The falls were submerged by the backwater of the Dalles Dam on March 16, 1957, disappearing forever under the tons of water that engulfed the area.

This reconstructed replica of Fort Clatsop is located a few miles southwest of Astoria. It stands as a monument to the Lewis and Clark Expedition which built it on the same site in 1805 as their winter headquarters.

Courtesy Oregon Department of Transportation

This mural depicts the scene of the Lewis and Clark Expedition at Celilo Falls in 1805

The Steamer *Beaver*

The *Beaver,* a small 101-foot vessel, was built for the Hudson's Bay Company in 1835 on the Thames River in London to be used for duties in the New World. She left English waters in August 1835 using sails as her motive power. Little was known of steam navigation so the Hudson's Bay Company decided to stow the thirteen-foot paddle wheels in the hold and sail the *Beaver* to the Northwest as a brig.

The first task upon the arrival of the *Beaver* in Oregon was to put her engines in running order. At Fort Vancouver (Washington) the ship's engineers and carpenter installed the paddle wheels and steamed up the boilers. It was May 31, 1836 when the little side-wheeler *Beaver* made her initial run on the Columbia to the mouth of the Willamette River. Several days later she chugged her way to the mouth of the Columbia, crossing over the bar into the ocean and was the first steamer on the Pacific Ocean.

SCHEDULE:

Left London, England, August 29, 1835.
Arrived Astoria, Oregon, April 4, 1836.

Left, the *Beaver* ran aground on some rocks near Vancouver, B.C. in July 1888. She remained for four years the object of curiosity for tourists and the object of concern to a few people who found it impossible to stir up enough interest to preserve the little steamer. In June 1892, the swell from a passing ocean liner caused one of the boilers on the stranded *Beaver* to break loose, causing her complete destruction.

The steamship *Beaver* — the first Pacific Ocean steamer, built in 1835

The *Star of Oregon*

On May 19, 1841 the first seagoing vessel built in the Oregon country slid quietly into the Willamette River from the east side of Swan Island, now a part of Portland. Today this location is a mass of industry and dry-dock repairs for oceangoing vessels.

Swan Island in 1841 was covered by a dense stand of oak trees from which the frame of this small 53-foot vessel was made. This little schooner, definitely not the most seaworthy, was named the *Star of Oregon*. It was built and sailed by a few hardy Americans who wanted to show the country, including the British Hudson's Bay Company, just what Americans could accomplish on their own.

The plan of the American shipbuilders, carried through to a brilliant consummation, was to build and sail their craft to California, then a Mexican possession, trade her for cattle and drive the stock overland back to Oregon. This is exactly what they accomplished.

SCHEDULE:

Left Cape Disappointment (mouth of the Columbia River), September 12, 1842.
Arrived San Francisco (then called Yerba Buena), September 17, 1842.

The *Star of Oregon*

Preparations for the day's travel ahead

Fixing a meal at the end of the day's journey

The Early Settlers

After the Lewis and Clark report covering the vast Oregon domain reached the American people, settlers began moving west clamoring "ON TO OREGON." The first to come were the trappers and mountain men looking for beaver, otter and other furbearing animals.

In 1843 a vast migration of settlers began moving from all parts of the United States into the Oregon country. A few came around the Horn, the southern-most part of South America, by ship. The majority came overland via the covered wagon using a four-wheeled vehicle of farm-wagon size and type strongly built for transportation of families and their belongings. The Oregon Trail and the Barlow Trail were names that became the word of the day.

The trip over the famous Oregon Trail starting from Independence, Missouri required better than four months to complete. Many of the early wagons were pulled by a pair of oxen rather than horses. Oxen were better able to stand the long trip. One ox would pull as much as two mules and in mud as much as four mules. Oxen will plunge through mud, swim over streams, drive into thickets and climb mountains to get at the grass and will eat almost anything.

A group of wagons traveling together was referred to as a wagon train. This was an organized caravan of from two to one hundred fifty rigs. There was safety in the larger wagon trains from Indian attacks. At night the wagons were drawn up into a circle end-to-end. This provided a corral for the horses, mules and oxen and a fortress for the people.

Taking a break in the day

Inside a covered wagon

Fording a river

Bourne Stage at Sumpter around 1900

High water — Express & Transfer to the rescue

Delivering milk in Portland in the snow

A freighting team between Arlington and Condon, Gilliam County

Studebaker advertisement

These two monthly publications were very influential in encouraging colonization and development of the West. Both issues were printed in 1905.

PEOPLE'S TRANSPORTATION CO.

The People's Transportation Co.'s Steamer **ALERT** will leave PORTLAND for OREGON CITY, **Every Morning** at 6½ o'clock, carrying the United States Mails. Returning—will leave for Portland at 1 P. M.

The Steamer **SENATOR** will leave OREGON CITY daily, (Sundays excepted) at 7 o'clock, A. M. Returning—will leave Portland at 2 o'clock, P. M.

The Steamer **RELIANCE** will leave CANEMAH every **Monday** and **Thursday** morning upon the arrival of the ALERT from Portland, for CORVALLIS and intermediate points.

The Steamer **FANNIE PATTON** will leave CANEMAH every **Thursday** and **Friday** for CORVALLIS and intermediate points.

The Steamers **ALBANY, SHOO FLY, ACTIVE** and **ECHO** will leave CANEMAH **ONCE A WEEK** for EUGENE CITY.

The Steamer **DAYTON** to DAYTON and McMINNVILLE **Every Monday, Wednesday** and **Friday.**

A. A. McCULLY,
President.

T. McF. PATTON, Sec'y,   (1871)

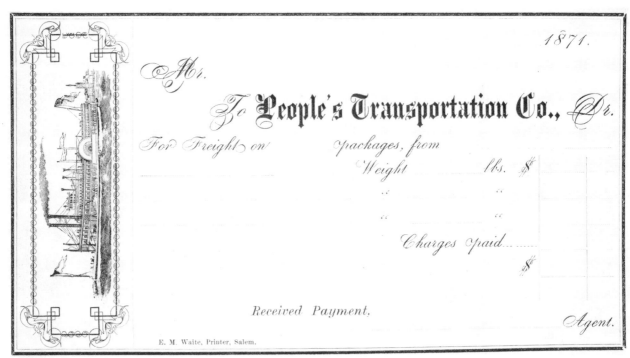

A Bill of Lading for the People's Transportation Company

The First Railroad in Oregon

The first horse drawn portage in the state was a very short piece of wooden tramway connecting Abernethys Island with the mainland at Oregon City built in 1846 by James McMillan. D. P. Thompson constructed a wooden-strap track along the same portage road in 1861 and the People's Transportation Company bought the portage line in 1865, laid iron rails and added a crane-like arrangement for lifting heavy cargo.

Following is an extract from Rev. Samuel Parker's *Journal of an Exploring Tour Beyond the Rocky Mountains:* "1865 Monday, June 5 clear and pleasant. Arose quite early; packed things for trip; ate breakfast; called at printing office (*Oregonian* where I had been setting type for more than a year); went down to the boat, anxiously awaiting the hour of departure up the river. Started at 7:00 A.M. on the *Senator* with Captain Pease as master; fare to Oregon City, one dollar; walked the portage; threw carpetbag on tram, drawn by a skinny, discouraged horse; went on the *Reliance* at Canemah; arrived in Salem at 6:30 P.M.; fare four dollars. Pleasant trip, though monotonous. Reading most of the time, saw a deer swimming in the river. Met friends."

Photo looking west shows the iron portage track with unloading dock near the front of Imperial Mills in Oregon City. It was the first railroad in Oregon, built in 1846. The water is known as Boat Basin and is used by steamers operating above Willamette Falls. The river boat (*right*) is under construction. This photo was taken in 1866.

A view overlooking Oregon City in 1866, looking south with the Willamette River and Falls in the background. The steamers shown in Boat Basin *(left)* are believed to belong to the People's Transportation Company running between Oregon City, Salem and Corvallis. The steamer shown *(right)* is one running between Oregon City, Portland and Vancouver below Willamette Falls. The large building *(center)* is the Oregon Manufacturing Company, a woolen mill. Directly in front of the mill is the original location and home of Dr. John McLoughlin, former chief factor for the Hudson's Bay Company and considered by many as the father of Oregon. The home was moved in 1909 to its present location at the top of Singer Hill. This photo was taken several years before the Oregon City Locks were opened.

The Baldwin Locomotive

Back in the days when American industry was young and untried, a discouraged jeweler looking about for a better trade formed a partnership with a machinist — and thereby one of the greatest locomotive factories in the world was born.

Matthias Baldwin, the jeweler, and David Mason, the toolmaker, didn't start out to make railroad engines, or any other kind of engines. Their plans initially covered book-binder's machinery and cylinders for the calico printers of New England cotton mills. Their first steam engine, a stationary vertical boiler, was born of necessity, for they needed a power plant for their new factory and it was easier to invent one than to buy it. The engine was such a success that engine building became the major activity of the company. Mason soon dropped out leaving Baldwin in charge.

Revenue Earners

It takes Modern Locomotives to make money these days!

THE BALDWIN LOCOMOTIVE WORKS
PHILADELPHIA

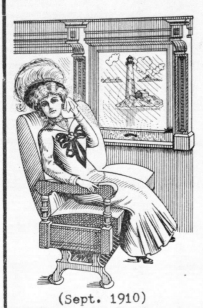
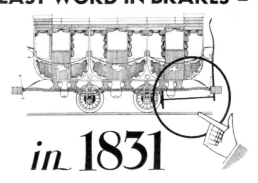
Early locomotive advertisements

CHRISTMAS ON THE OVERLAND ROUTE

Oregon Boundary Question Ratified

The front page of the *Oregon Spectator,* Vol. I No. 21 of November 12, 1846, advised that the United States Senate had ratified the treaty covering the Oregon boundary question. There was no wire or telegraph service at that date and this information was secured from a New York newspaper of June 18 that had just reached them.

The *Oregon Spectator* was published in Oregon City from 1846 until 1855. It was Oregon's first newspaper and the first on the entire Pacific Coast. It was fifteen by eleven inches in size, had four pages, four columns to the page and it came out every other week.

The Oregon Spectator, Oregon's first newspaper and first on the entire Pacific Coast, reports the ratification of the treaty settling the Oregon boundary question.

Portland, Oregon — Off
for the beach.

The last day of the season

At the beach on the west
shore.

The Beautiful Columbia

The Columbia River was once called "the Oregon." This is the river which Bryant mentions in his immortal poem, *Thanatopsis:*

Or lose thyself in the continuous woods,
Where rolls the Oregon, and hears no sound,
Save his own dashings — yet the dead are there.

The navigable rivers of Oregon were the roadways for the early explorers of the West. If the magnitude of the Columbia River system could be stretched in one continuous line from its mouth eastward, ships could start from Astoria and land their cargo at the docks in St. Paul, Minnesota; or stretching in a southerly direction, could traverse the country from Portland to New Orleans. From 1850 to about 1870 the waterways with their steamboats dominated the state transportation system both along the rivers and coastwise service.

Come with us and enjoy the Pacific Ocean and the beautiful Oregon beaches.

Through the streets of Portland from all directions come well-laden hacks with scores of happy looking people ready to board a stern-wheeler steamboat for a trip down the Columbia River to Astoria and the Coast.

The warning whistle blows and a number of people with their baggage have arrived at the very last moment. The starting whistle blows, the gangway is pulled on board, the bell from the bridge to the engine room rings, the ropes are thrown off the docks, the paddle wheels begin to turn, and we are off. . . .

Our friends wave to us as we pull away from the dock.

It is shortly after 7:00 A.M. and the *S. G. Reed* cuts through the water as gracefully as a swan. We journey down the Willamette River through the Portland Harbor district for a few miles and then join the Columbia River for the remainder of our trip.

After riding for seven or eight hours on

OREGON RAILWAY AND NAVIGATION CO.

RIVER DIVISION.
(1882)

LOWER COLUMBIA RIVER.

Portland to Astoria.

DAYS.	Mondays, Wednesdays Fridays.	Tuesdays, Thursdays, Saturday.
STEAMERS.	R. R. Thompson.	S. G. Reed.
Leave Portland	6 00 A. M.	6 00 A. M.
" St. Helens	7 45 "	8 00 "
" Kalama	8 30 "	9 00 "
" Rainier	9 00 "	9 45 "
" Oak Point	10 00 "	
" West Port		12 15 P. M.
" Cathlamet	11 15 "	
" Clifton		1 00 "
" Skomockawa	11 45 "	
" Brookfield	12 15 P.M.	
" Knappa		2 30 "
Arrive Astoria	1 30 P.M.	3 30 P. M.

Steamers connect at Astoria for Ilwaco, Fort Stevens and Canby.

Astoria to Portland.

Making direct connection with the Overland Train for the East.

DAYS.	Mondays, Wednesdays Friday.	Tuesdays Thursdays, Saturdays.
STEAMERS.	S. G. Reed.	R. R. Thompson.
Leave Astoria	6 00 A. M.	6 00 A. M.
" Knappa	7 00 "	
" Brookfield		7 45 "
" Skomockawa		7 15 "
" Clifton	8 30 "	
" Cathlamet		8 15 "
" West Port	9 20 "	
" Oak Point		9 30 "
" Rainier		10 30 "
" Kalama	12 30 P. M.	11 00 "
" St. Helens	1 45 "	12 00 M.
Arrive Portland	4 00 P. M.	2 00 P. M.

Steamer travel schedule for the Lower Columbia River

the smooth riding vessel and enjoying the interesting scenes along the river we reach Astoria. Some of our crowd continue on to Ilwaco Landing on the Washington side of the river for a trip to the North Beaches on the narrow gauge railroad. The rest of us board the *Steamer Electric* from Fishers Dock in Astoria for a short trip to Skipanon where we connect with the horse drawn stages for an eighteen-mile trip to Seaside along the Pacific Ocean.

Above, the *S.G. Reed* in the Lower Columbia River

Left, inside the dining area of the *S.G. Reed*

Right, inside the *S.G. Reed*

The Seaside House

The Seaside House was built in June 1873 by Ben Holladay, transportation tycoon. Its location today would be on the city golf course. Holladay entertained royalty, politicians, railroad barons and almost anyone that could be of financial help to Holladay himself. He entertained with a lavishness rarely seen in this pioneer state. It had a little bit of the grandeur from Europe, the French cuisine being unexcelled and entertainment of all sorts: gambling, fishing, hunting, horses; it had everything. Eleven months later the Seaside House was sold to Charles H. Dexter, formerly of the Cliff House in San Francisco. It eventually became city property used as a hospital and was torn down in 1922.

THE SEASIDE HOUSE, CLATSOP BEACH.

C. H. DEXTER,

FORMERLY OF THE "CLIFF HOUSE," SAN FRANCISCO,

Announces to his friends and the public that he has leased the New and Elegant Hotel recently erected. The house is elegantly furnished, and possesses all modern improvements. A large and Spacious DINING ROOM, BILLIARD ROOM, EXTENSIVE PARLORS, BATH ROOMS, ETC., ETC. A half-mile Race Track, with Shell drive; Croquet Ground. Children's Play Grounds, Etc., Etc. Boats upon the creek; plenty of Trout Fishing; a splendid Stable, with Saddle Horses for those who wish for Equestrian Rides over the Beach; Bathing Houses for Salt Water Bathing, and, in fact, everything necessary for the Pleasure Seeker, the Tourist or the Invalid. The Table will be unexcelled, and the subscriber pledges himself that nothing will be left undone for the pleasure and comfort of his Patrons. Terms moderate and satisfactory. The Hotel will be open for the reception of Guests May 1st, 1874. CHARLES H. DEXTER.

Announcement of the opening of The Seaside House, Clatsop Beach, in 1874

Courtesy Oregon Historical Society

The famous Seaside House in Seaside, Oregon. The stage from Astoria has just arrived. Many of these patrons used the steamboat from Portland.

At the beach

Advertising the initial trip of steamer *Hassalo*

NORTH BEACH
—WASHINGTON—
AS A SUMMER RESORT IS
UNEQUALED

The thriving hamlets along its eighteen miles of Natural Boulevard are better prepared than ever this season to entertain visitors.

INITIAL TRIP OF STEAMER

"Hassalo"

SATURDAY, JUNE 1st

To ASTORIA and MEGLER

Leaving Ash Street Dock
1 P. M.

Service thereafter daily except Saturday and Sunday, at 8 A. M., and on Saturdays at 1 P. M. Steamer "Harvest Queen" will leave daily except Saturday and Sunday at 8 P. M., and on Saturdays at 10 P. M.

The "Hassalo" has been re-built and re-fitted throughout. Her new engines make her the swiftest steamer on the Columbia, and with her many other additions and changes is prepared to handle the best class of travel.

Trains meet all boats at Megler for
North Beach Points.

Excellent Restaurant Service   Meals a la Carte
State-room reservations can be made at Ash Street Dock

City Ticket Office
THIRD AND WASHINGTON STREETS
(1912)   Portland

Ilwaco Railway & Navigation Company narrow gauge line operating in Washington from Megler to Nahacotta, a distance of twenty-eight miles, pulled by a 2-6-0 Baldwin.

The *Harvest Queen* at St. Helens

The *Bailey Gatzert (left)*, 177 feet long, built in 1890, and the *Charles R. Spencer (right)*, 234 feet long, built in 1901

WHITE COLLAR LINE

Str. "BAILEY GATZERT"

DAILY ROUND TRIP—EXCEPT MONDAY

Vancouver, Cascade Locks, St. Martin's Springs, Hood River,
White Salmon, Lyle and The Dalles

═══ TIME CARD ═══

Leave Portland...............7 : 00 A. M.	Leave The Dalles............4 : 00 P. M.
Arrive The Dalles...........3 : 00 P. M.	Arrive Portland............. .10 : 00 P. M.

....MEALS THE VERY BEST....

Sunday Trips a Leading Feature.
This Route has the Grandest Scenic Attractions on Earth.
LANDING FOOT OF ALDER ST.
BOTH PHONES, MAIN 351

OREGON AGENTS.	WASHINGTON AGENTS.
E. W. CRICHTON, Portland.	ETHEL MCGURN, Vancouver.
PRATHER & BARNES, Hood River.	J. C. WYATT, Vancouver
JOHN M. FILLOON, The Dalles.	WOLFORD & WYERS, White Salmon

1910

Up the Columbia to The Dalles

In 1910, a trip up the Columbia River was a wonderful way to spend a Sunday. After the Cascade Locks was built, the trip was made much quicker, especially since the portage line no longer had to be used.

Summertime excursionists swarmed aboard the stern-wheelers by the hundreds, each bustling to get the choicest seat from which to see the river and the passing scenery. At midday picnic baskets were opened by those who had brought them and the ship's dining room was used for those who had not. The Cascade Locks and Canal were completely submerged in 1938 by the backed up waters of Bonneville Dam.

Map and schedules of steamer travels on the Columbia River

SAN FRANCISCO
AND
NEW YORK
THROUGH LINE
Via Isthmus of Panama.

Steamers leave San Francisco on the 3d, 13th and 23d of each month for Panama, via way ports (as per page 2), connecting at Aspinwall (Colon) with Company's Steamers due in New York on the 3d, 11th and 21st respectively.

No Tickets issued for points in the United States beyond the port of New York.

RATES OF FARE:
(Subject to change without notice.)

Cabin, $ *120 00*

Steerage, $ *40 00*

(No Intermediate Class.)

Children between 6 and 12 years, half fare; between 2 and 6 years, quarter fare; under 2 years, free.

Servants accompanying their employers will be charged two-thirds of Cabin rates, without regard to age or sex, and will be berthed and served with meals according to ship's regulations.

These rates include railroad fare across the Isthmus of Panama; also, berths, meals, and medical attendance.

100 lbs. of baggage allowed to each Cabin passenger.
150   "   "   "   " Steerage "

Proportionate allowance to Children.

Excess Baggage 10 cents per pound. Merchandise, Bedding, etc., will not be taken as Baggage; when carried as freight will be charged 5 cents per pound, prepaid.

San Francisco, June 1st 1893.

PACIFIC MAIL
STEAMSHIP COMPANY
FOR
NEW YORK, MEXICO
CENTRAL AMERICA
AND
ISTHMUS OF PANAMA
Connecting at Panama with Steamers for Ports on
WEST COAST OF SOUTH AMERICA
And at Aspinwall (Colon) with Steamers for the
WEST INDIES, HAVANA AND
EUROPE.

☞ Prompt attention paid to Written or Telegraphic Reservation of State Rooms or Berths, which should be engaged at least one week before sailing. Cabin plans on exhibition and passage tickets for sale at the

COMPANY'S OFFICE,
FIRST AND BRANNAN STREETS, SAN FRANCISCO

ALEXANDER CENTER,
General Agent.

Pacific Mail Steamship Company poster and advertisements

1893 San Francisco to New York — water trip, twenty-five days, 5,220 miles

Lv. Portland

Ar. San Francisco — three-day trip, 639 miles

Lv. San Francisco

Ar. Panama — fifteen-day trip

Lv. Panama on Panama Railroad

Ar. Aspinwall (Colon) — forty-seven mile trip and made in one day crossing Isthmus of Panama

Lv. Aspinwall (Colon)

Ar. New York — nine-day trip, 1,975 miles

The Panama Railroad ran from Panama to Aspinwall (now called Colon) across the Isthmus of Panama, a forty-seven-mile trip.

Oregon Becomes A State

The state of Oregon was born on Valentine's Day, February 14, 1859. Congress by a margin of eleven votes passed the statehood bill on February 12 and President James Buchanan signed it into law two days later making Oregon the thirty-third state to join the Union.

Statehood came only after considerable debate from both within and without the territory. It was discussed in the disruptive shadows of the forthcoming war between the states and debated by both Congress and Oregonians at home.

Representatives from the home state were anxious that the good tidings about statehood reach Oregon as soon as possible.

Febuary 14, 1859: Oregon became a state.

It was telegraphed to St. Louis, Missouri. The news left St. Louis on John Butterfield's Great Overland Mail Stage for San Francisco, a distance of 2,650 miles. The stage was routed via Little Rock, El Paso, Yuma, Los Angeles, and into San Francisco.

March 10, 1859: The stage arrived in San Francisco.

March 11, 1859: It left San Francisco on the steamship *Brother Jonathan* for Portland, Oregon.

March 15, 1859: The steamship arrived in Portland, Oregon.

March 16, 1859: Steffen Senter, a resident of Canemah, Oregon, rode his pony for thirty hours to bring the good news to Salem, the capital of the state.

The Butterfield Stage

The message that Oregon had become a state was hurried to the mail clerk aboard the *Brother Jonathan*, a 220-foot oceangoing side-wheeler, on March 10, 1859 in San Francisco. The next day Capt. George Staples took the *Brother Jonathan* through the Golden Gate and headed northward through a rough sea, but under a full head of steam and a press of canvas. At 4:00 P.M. on the afternoon of March 14, the ship stood off the Columbia River bar and twelve hours later was docking in Portland.

Courtesy Oregon State Highway

This mural, which hangs behind the president's desk in the State Senate chambers in Salem, depicts the scene on March 17, 1859, when word was received that Oregon had been accepted into the Union. Steffen Senter *(center, holding his horse)* rode thirty hours on his pony from Oregon City to bring this news to Salem. The man on horseback *(left)* is John Whiteaker, Oregon's first governor. As there was no state capitol building or Supreme Court building at that time, both met in the Bennett House, Salem's swank frame hostelry owned by Capt. Charles Bennett, a former riverman who is credited with being the first man to discover gold in California. The Bennett House was located at High and State Streets, where the Ben Franklin Savings and Loan occupies this location today. As most of the important political events took place at the Bennett House (they were called houses in those days rather than hotels), Frank W. Schwartz, the artist, has included it in the mural.

THE WEEKLY  OREGONIAN.

EQUAL RIGHTS, EQUAL LAWS, AND EQUAL JUSTICE TO ALL MEN.

DRYER, PROPRIETOR.   PORTLAND, OREGON, SATURDAY, MARCH 19, 1859.   VOL. IX.---NO. 17.

This issue of *The Oregonian* belatedly told readers that the state of Oregon had been admitted to the Union. It also carried a leading editorial denouncing Oregon's first U.S. senators, Joseph Lane and Delazon Smith and its first representative, Lafayette Grover, for their part in bringing statehood about. They had misrepresented Oregon's population as ninety-three thousand when it was actually only forty-five thousand, said *The Oregonian:* "We are smuggled into the Union upon the exaggerated statements of Grover, Smith and Lane. No state except Oregon has ever been admitted into the Union without some provision being made or at least an evidence of the power and ability to support and sustain itself. We have no capital, no public buildings, no library, no revenue and no provision for the support of a State Government . . ."

Stopping to unload the U.S. Mail along with passengers in front of the Grants Pass Post Office

Way-Bills kept by the California and Oregon United States Mail Line in 1857

Stage Travel

Oregon was growing in the 1860s and needed transportation, especially into California. Waterways served as a means of transportation but many were fearful of this type of travel. The packhorse had its difficulties due to hostile Indians, bad weather and difficult terrain. However, early settlers in isolated areas owed many of the few comforts and necessities they possessed to the courage and determination of the packtrain operators.

Mountains in Southern Oregon were a treacherous portion of the trip between Portland and Sacramento. Following much agitation a private toll road was built across sections of the Siskiyou Mountains after the Oregon legislature approved the measure in 1857-58.

In 1860 the road was completed and daily stage operation to California was started, taking seven days from April 1 to December 1 and twelve days for the balance of the year.

In 1866 we must have felt we were living in a wonderful age. It was now possible to go by stage from Portland to Sacramento in six days. At 6:00 A.M. each day one or two pair of horses threw their weight against their collars to pull a wooden-wheeled Concord stagecoach from the Arrigoni Hotel at Front and Stark Streets in Portland onto the Stark Street Ferry to cross the Willamette River and then roll south to California.

A government contract for delivery of the U.S. Mails was awarded to The Oregon Stage Company amounting to ninety thousand dollars per annum. Each driver was instructed to keep a way-bill of his departures and arrivals, including names of all passengers making the trip. This type of service continued until the railroad was in operation between the two states.

A toll road owned by Henry Clay Dollarhide some time after the Oregon legislature authorized the building of toll roads in 1857–58. The stage companies paid to use the roads, as did wagon trains, horseback riders and those with sheep and cattle.

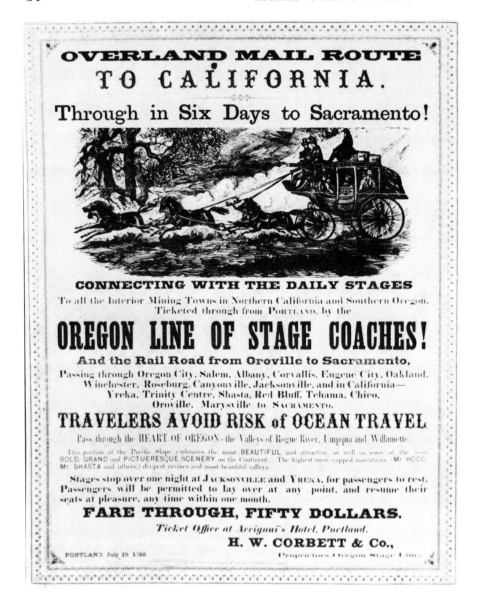

A poster published in 1866 by Henry Winslow Corbett three years after he purchased the 710-mile Oregon Stage Line. The poster was published after the tragic loss of the steamship *Brother Jonathan* where some two hundred lives were lost at sea on its sailing between San Francisco and Portland. Corbett thus emphasized in his advertisement the safety of land travel. Corbett became a U.S. senator from Oregon several years later.

A receipt prepared in advance by W. P. Mayhew, agent for the Oregon Stage Company signed by R. Barney for his services as hostler and his board during the month. He was probably paid in gold. A U.S. Federal tax stamp was affixed and cancelled using the initials of the payee.

Lv. Portland	July 1, 1867	6:00 A.M.
Ar. Oregon City		8:40 A.M.
Lv. Oregon City		8:50 A.M.
Ar. Salem		3:45 P.M.
Lv. Salem		4:00 P.M.
Ar. Albany		8:10 P.M.
Lv. Albany		8:30 P.M.
Ar. Corvallis		9:45 P.M.
Lv. Corvallis		10:00 P.M.
Ar. Eugene	July 2nd	6:00 A.M.
Lv. Eugene		6:30 A.M.
Ar. Oakland		6:25 P.M.
Lv. Oakland		7:15 P.M.
Ar. Roseburg		10:10 P.M.
Lv. Roseburg		10:35 P.M.
Ar. Canyonville	July 3rd	5:30 A.M.
Lv. Canyonville		6:00 A.M.
Ar. Jacksonville		9:30 A.M.
Lv. Jacksonville	July 4th	3:30 A.M.

"Third-class passengers, get behind and push"

An advertisement from the Portland Directory

Driver Al Beard stops his matched team beside the Metropolitan Hotel in Roseburg in 1877

ADVICE FOR STAGE TRAVELER: (1870)

1. In cold weather don't ride with tight boots, shoes or gloves.

2. When the driver asks you to get off and walk, do so without grumbling. He won't request it unless absolutely necessary.

3. If the team runs away, sit still and take your chances. If you jump, nine chances out of ten you will get hurt.

4. In very cold weather abstain entirely from liquor when on the road because you will freeze twice as fast under its influence.

5. Spit on the leeward side.

6. Don't swear or lop over on your neighbors when sleeping.

7. Never shoot on the road as the noise may frighten the horses.

8. Don't discuss politics or religion.

9. Don't point out where murders have been committed, especially if women are present as passengers.

10. Don't grease your hair because travel is dusty.

11. DON'T IMAGINE FOR A MINUTE THAT YOU ARE GOING ON A PICNIC. EXPECT ANNOYANCES, DISCOMFORT AND SOME REAL HARDSHIPS.

Coles Station at the California-Oregon state line. This was the last stage to leave from here prior to the opening of the Southern Pacific line on December 17, 1887 between San Franciso and Portland.

Transportation via stagecoach

WAY FARES FORWARDED.		DATE.	AMOUNT.	DRIVER.
From Oregon City	to Yreka	*Odenton* July 1	2 50	*Shepard*
" Salem	" "	"	00	*Hosting*
" Albany	" "	" 15	8 50	
" Corvallis	" "	" 1		
" Eugene City	" "	" 2	8 50	*Mullen*
" Oakland	" "	" 2	11 50	*Pane*
" Roseburg	" "			
" Canyonville	" "	" 3	25 50	*Carll*
" Jacksonville	" "	" 4		*L. B. Tucker*

Way Fares Forwarded, from Oregon City to Yreka

A typical stage depot of past years

Two of the leading express agents of the 1860s

The Concord Coach

"Second perhaps only to Mr. Colt's revolvers as an influence in the West was the Concord coach, America's most romantic piece of rolling stock," according to Stewart Holbrook, a famous Oregon historical writer. Further he stated, "both the gun and the vehicle have so permeated the legend of the Old West that no story in pulp or celluloid is complete without them."

The perfectionists who devised this classic coach were Lewis Downing and J. Stephen Abbot who at Concord, New Hampshire in 1826 formed a partnership that was to endure for one hundred and two years during which they turned out more than three thousand vehicles. The care began in the woods where either an Abbot or a Downing selected the best trees of white ash or oak. The elm for the hubs got the same treatment. The panels were of prime basswood and were cured by the slow process of clamping their edges around a form, then placing them in front of an open

A Concord stage en route to Mill City, Detroit stops at Turner, Oregon in front of the Hotel Baker. Elijah C. and Sara O. Baker can be seen standing in front of the hotel.

fire where they were intermittently moist-
ened until properly shaped.

The coach was built to provide comfort
for the passengers and withstand the abuse
it had to take on the rough western roads.
The body of the coach had a rolling motion
far more comfortable for its occupants than
the jolting of a wagon.

The company's peak came on the 15th of
April when a train load of stages was shipped
by the Concord people to Wells Fargo &
Company to be used in the West.

The stage line carried the Wells Fargo
Bank funds, U.S. Mail and passengers from
Sacramento to Portland and back and the
company payroll named thirty-five drivers,
seventy-five hostlers and fourteen agents.
Inventory included sixty route stations,
twenty-eight coaches and five hundred
horses.

A standard Concord would carry fifteen
passengers while larger ones would seat
thirty-one passengers. At the coming of the
railroad, stages were used for feeder or connection service to non-rail points.

Some of the Concord Coaches used so plentifully in the early development of the West

The use of our Coaches and Wagons on all the Mail routes in America and the English Colonies is a guarantee of their superiority.

All our lumber is carefully seasoned to meet the requirements of a dry climate, and all parts—including axles and springs—being made within our works, are reliable. The setting of the Axletree has given our Coaches a reputation for ease of draught.

Parties ordering will be particular to name width of track, measuring from outside of one wheel to the inside of the other on the ground.

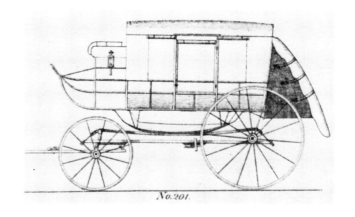

Mail Coach, with leather boots, deck seat, brake, lamps, and ornamented sides.

To seat 12 inside,		$1,000
" 9 " (heavy,)		900
" 9 " (medium,)		850
2 seats, 3 on a side,—or 3 seats, 2 on a side,—to seat 6 inside,		750
ADD		
For deck seat on rear of coach,		20
" packing body only,		12
" " coach complete,		20
DEDUCT		
If no lamps,		7
" deck seat,		20
" ornamental paint,		20

Illustrations of the Concord Coach from the Abbot and Downing catalog in 1873 showing various types and costs.

Steamship *George W. Elder* taken in 1905 at Goble, Oregon on the Columbia River. This ship was built in Chester, Pennsylvania in 1847 and was brought to Oregon in 1876. It was 250 feet long and carried 125 first-class and 200 steerage passengers.

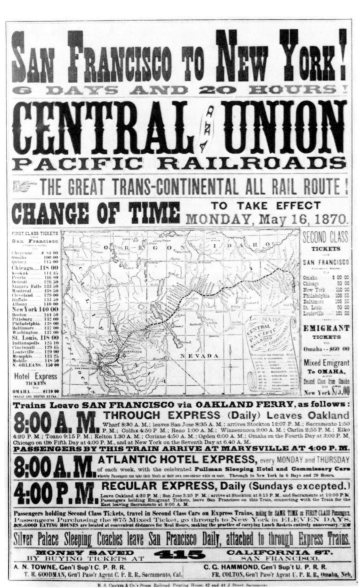

Central and Union Pacific Railroad's schedule advertisement

An advertisement that appeared in 1870 railroad public time-tables.

Congressman John Whiteaker Goes East In A Hurry

In 1879 John Lycurgus Whiteaker (1820–1902), Oregon's first governor serving from 1859 to 1862, was the newly elected congressman from Oregon.

On March 7 his sleep was rudely interrupted at his home in Lane County near Eugene. He was told his presence was urgently needed to answer roll call in Washington, D.C. on March 18 at the special session of Congress to assure election of Samuel G. Randall to the speakership of the House of Representatives. Party leaders bent on electing a speaker of the House favorable to their programs discovered that one more vote was needed for the election on this date.

In 1879 transcontinental train service to the Northwest had not been completed. Traveling to California meant using the train to Roseberg, the end of the line, then by stage to Redding, California and again by train to Sacramento.

The ex-governor and newly elected congressman decided to use rail from Eugene to Portland, steamer to San Francisco, and go east on the newly completed transcontinental Central Pacific-Union Pacific Railroad.

The bar at Astoria was so rough the ship was unable to cross from the Columbia River into the Pacific Ocean. Whiteaker wired National Headquarters telling them of the delay. Back came a reply advising that the party would operate a special train from San Francisco to insure his being on hand in Washington.

John Lycurgus Whiteaker, Oregon's first governor

On March 10 the steamship *George W. Elder* was able to cross the bar at Astoria resulting in a twenty-four hour delay from the original schedule. The ship arrived in San Francisco the morning of March 12. Whiteaker was met and hurried across the bay to Oakland to a waiting eastbound special train. The train arrived in Washington, D.C. on March 17 on a five day, five hour and eleven minute train schedule, setting a new cross-country speed record.

SCHEDULE:

Lv. Eugene	Oregon & California No. 15 Oregon Express	4:45 A.M.	March 8, 1879	Saturday
Ar. Portland	Oregon & California No. 15 Oregon Express	10:40 A.M.	March 8, 1879	Saturday
Lv. Portland	SS *George W. Elder*	12:00 P.M.	March 8, 1879	Saturday
Ar. Astoria	SS *George W. Elder*	A.M.	March 9, 1879	Sunday
Lv. Astoria	SS *George W. Elder*	A.M.	March 10, 1879	Monday
Ar. San Francisco	SS *George W. Elder*	A.M.	March 12, 1879	Wednesday
Lv. San Francisco	Central Pacific Special Train	A.M.	March 12, 1879	Wednesday
Ar. Washington, D.C.	Central Pacific Special Train		March 17, 1879	Monday

SOUTHERN PACIFIC LINES

THE SOUTHERN PACIFIC RAILROAD had its beginning in the Central Pacific Railroad (CP) which built the western link of the first transcontinental railroad. Pushing eastward from Sacramento in 1863 the Central Pacific met the westward building Union Pacific (UP) at Promontory Point, Utah where the historic last spike was driven May 10, 1863. The line was built over and through the rock walls of the Sierra Nevada mountains and across the desert with rail and primitive locomotive brought by sailing ships "around the Horn."

The events which led up to SP's acquisition of the first major rail line in Oregon makes for an interesting story.

The following excerpt was taken from the Portland City Directory in 1870: "During the past year, two lines of railroad have been projected in Oregon: The Oregon Central Railroad (East Side), running from Portland along the east bank of the Willamette River to Eugene City in Lane County, a distance of one hundred and twenty-five miles. This line designs to traverse through Clackamas, Marion, Linn, Benton and Lane counties. The Oregon Central Railroad (West Side) contemplates starting from Portland and running along the west bank of the Willamette River to some point at the head of the Willamette Valley, traversing through Washington, Yamhill, Polk, Benton and Lane counties. Both companies are vigorously at work grading track, building bridges and culverts, erecting shops for machinery and otherwise making suitable

preparations to complete their undertaking prior to the arrival of rolling stock and rails now en route from the Eastern states. Both lines give employment to large numbers of employees and when both are completed

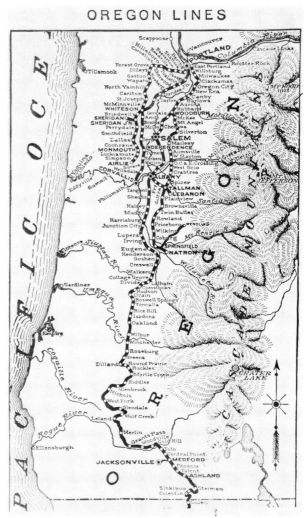

Oregon lines between the Pacific shore and the Cascade Mountains.

An early Central Pacific passenger train making a stop at a scenic point somewhere in the Sierras allowing the brakes to cool off and permitting the passengers to detrain and secure a better view. Note the rear observation open car of that time.

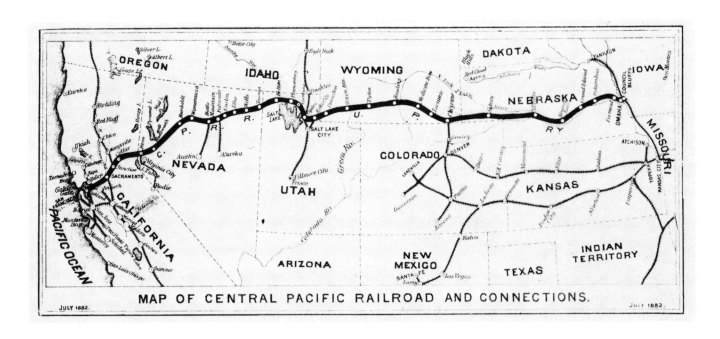

MAP OF CENTRAL PACIFIC RAILROAD AND CONNECTIONS.

their success will add materially to the agriculture and commercial wants of the entire state. Other lines are spoken of but as yet these are the only two extensive lines that have gone to work having in view practical results."

A bitter legal and political tussle was underway when Ben Holladay, a colorful westerner fresh from lucrative exploits with stagecoach and steamship ventures, cast his lot with the "East Side" company. Eventually he also gained control of the "West Side" line as well.

Holladay had obtained substantial backing from capitalists in Germany and had reorganized his entire railroad enterprise as The Oregon & California Railroad Company (O&C).

O&C trains were in operation to Salem, Albany and Eugene by 1871. The rail line reached Roseburg on December 3, 1872 and

at this point construction was halted for nine years. Holladay failed financially. Traffic revenue from the sparsely settled region was not sufficient to meet expenses and when interest on the bonds could not be met in 1873, Holladay was forced out and the property was taken over by the German investors.

The German bondholders sent Henry Villard to take over and look after their interests.

Construction was resumed on the Oregon & California Railroad in 1881. The line reached Ashland May 4, 1884. Villard too had financial troubles and his regime crashed. The O&C Railroad was forced into receivership and on July 1, 1887 the properties were formally acquired under lease and later purchased by the Southern Pacific Company.

This is the "C. P. Huntington," Southern Pacific's No. 1 locomotive. It is one of the pioneer engines of the Central Pacific that was brought around Cape Horn by boat in 1864. This engine is a wood burner (4-2-4) and could haul four cars weighing twenty-two tons each at thirty-five miles per hour up a grade of twenty-six feet to the mile. It is now preserved as a relic and stored in Sacramento.

This is a Central Pacific freight train on a downhill grade. If the train begins to roll too fast the engineer will whistle for "down-brakes" — a succession of short sounds of the engine's whistle. The brakeman will run the length of the moving train turning or screwing the wheel-like apparatus shown above each boxcar. Brakemen carried brake-sticks which helped them with this duty; thus the term "brakemen." Being a brakeman was an easy enough job to learn but the main problem was staying alive to enjoy it. This photo was taken in the 1880s before the days of air brakes. Note that this train is a "double-header on the point" which means it has two engines that burned wood that had to be replaced about every twenty miles. These freight cars had the capacity of about ten tons.

Oregon Central Railroad engine No. 3, the "J. P. Stephens" (4-4-0 wood burning Hinkley locomotive), shown crossing the newly completed Clackamas River bridge. Construction of this 380-foot structure was the biggest single job in building the first twenty miles of railroad south from Portland. Flood waters harassed the builders and only through supreme effort was the structure completed in order to have the first twenty miles of track in operation by Christmas Day 1869 — the date required of the Oregon Central to qualify for the U.S. Federal Land Grant.

Much of the building of railroad right-of-ways in the 1860s and 1870s was done with pick and shovels while the dirt was removed in wheel scrapers.

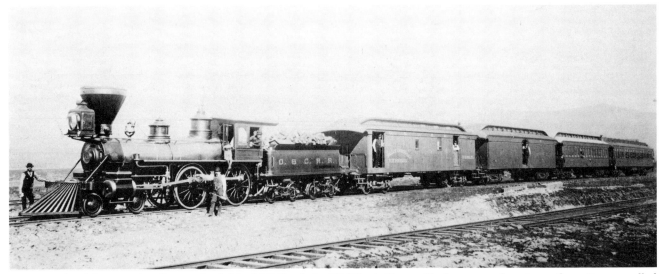

Oregon and California Railroad's train (probably O&C No. 1, the "California Express") taken somewhere in southern Oregon pulled by engine No. 22 (4-4-0 wood burner). Engineer D. McCarthy can be seen on the ground with an oil can while Fireman James Porter is leaning on the pilot bar. Both men have white shirts on which is almost unbelievable. The man in the cab is Joe Marshall, an engine wiper from Ashland. The small boy sitting on the running board is the engineer's son, H. G. McCarthy, who years later became an SP trainmaster.

Kerosene lamps, sheet iron stoves and straight backed, hard seats were common characteristics of the early coaches of the 1860s and 1870s.

Above, the Oregon Central Railroad "East Siders" drive the first spike in East Portland on April 16, 1868 near the dividing line between The Stephens and Tibbets claims, today known as Division Street. The first spike was driven by Rev. Josiah L. Parrish of Salem, one of the early Methodist Missionaries who came to Oregon traveling by ship around the Horn in the four hundred-ton *Lausanne*. Photo by Joseph Buchtel using an early French camera.

OFFICE OF
Oregon Central Railroad Company,
Salem, APRIL 8TH, 1868.

Mr. T. C. Shaw

You are respectfully invited to be present at the Breaking of Ground for the Oregon Central Railroad, which will take place at East Portland, on Thursday, April 16th, 1868, at 11 o'clock, A. M.

We are happy to inform you that the important work to be then commenced will be vigorously prosecuted.

By order of the Board of Directors.

S. A. Clarke
Secretary O. C. R. R. Co.

N. B.—The P. T. Co. will convey passengers to and from Portland, who desire to attend the celebration, at half the usual rates. A boat will go down the river from Salem on Wednesday, and return on Friday, for this purpose.

Left, Thomas Clemens Shaw of Salem was given an invitation to attend the Oregon Central Railroad's ground-breaking ceremonies. The People's Transportation Company offered steamboat services for half the usual fare for Salem people attending.

Office of the Oregon Central Rail Road Co
Salem Oregon December 30th 1869

It is hereby certified that Thaddeus R. Brooks is the chief engineer of the Oregon Central Rail Road, and that the location of the road, as represented on this map, is correct and approved by the company; and also that the said portion of the said road, extending southerly from the initial point a distance of Twenty miles and four hundred feet, and traced in lines of Blue, has been completed and equipped in all respects as required by law.

I. R. Moores
President

Attest
Geo. E. Cole
Secretary

On this page is the map and certificate of completion verifying the completion of the first twenty miles of track of the Oregon Central Railroad, starting from east Portland and extending south to a location then known as Parrot Creek, now called New Era. The document *(above)* is signed by Issac R. Moores, president of the Oregon Central Railroad and Salem resident, who then forwarded the certificate and map to the Governor of Oregon, George L. Woods. The following day the governor acknowledged receipt of the map and so advised the Oregon Central People. (See document opposite page.) By completing the first twenty miles of track within the prescribed time limit the railroad company qualified for a U.S. Federal Land Grant which consisted of alternating sections of land extending twenty miles from the track on each side, which could be sold and used for the payment of the line.

Executive Office

Salem Oregon December 31st 1869

I George L. Woods. Governor of the State of Oregon do hereby certify that this plat or map of the Oregon Central Rail Road has been duly filed in my office by the said Oregon Central Rail Road Company and shows that portion of the said railroad commencing in East Portland and ending near the mouth of Parrott Creek in Clackamas County Oregon a distance of Twenty miles and traced in lines of Blue, which has been completed and equipped as required by the Act of Congress approved July 25 1866 and amendments thereto, and the Act of the Legislative Assembly of the State of Oregon approved October October 20th 1868 granting lands to the said railroad Company

In testimony whereof. I have hereunto set my hand and caused to be affixed the Seal of the State of Oregon, the day and date above written

Geo. L. Woods
Governor of Or.

By the Governor.

Samuel E. May.
Secretary of State.

"Ten minutes for lunch" (less if the train is late or the conductor is in a bad mood). Not so long ago, when a person set out on a train journey that was to extend through the meal period he carried a "shoebox lunch or some other form of snack for the road. On some lines the trains stopped for meals as is depicted in this advertisement of 1884. Timetables showed such remarks as "twenty minute stop for supper" opposite schedules. Then came the diner — catering at first to the drawing room trade, the dining car service soon became a luxury enjoyed by everyone.

On June 28, 1884, the Raymond Excursion Party, which toured the entire country, climbed off the "California Express" (O&C No. 2) to allow an early Portland photographer (Partridge) to take this photograph. The picture was taken at the crossing of Twelfth and Court Streets, now one of the busiest corners in Salem. The trip was made before the line between San Francisco and Portland was completed, with a portion of the trip made by stage. Notice the back side of the capitol building, without a dome, in the background.

1884 SCHEDULE:

Lv. San Francisco	SP No. 20-4 Oregon Express	4:00 P.M.	Monday
Ar. Hornbrook, California	SP No. 20-4 Oregon Express	9:30 A.M.	Tuesday
Lv. Hornbrook, California	California, Oregon & Idaho Stage Co.	10:00 A.M.	Tuesday
Ar. Ashland	California, Oregon & Idaho Stage Co.	4:30 P.M.	Tuesday
Lv. Ashland	O&C No. 2 California Express	5:00 P.M.	Tuesday
Ar. Salem	O&C No. 2 California Express	7:34 A.M.	Wednesday
Ar. Portland	O&C No. 2 California Express	10:10 A.M.	Wednesday

Oregon Pacific No. 1, the "Yaquina Local," ready to leave Yaquina City in 1888 pulled by locomotive No. 4 (4-4-0 wood burner). Boat patrons who boarded the *S.S. Willamette Valley (left)* in San Francisco for Yaquina City in Oregon are now using the train to continue their trip into the valley. The two men nearest to the engine are Superintendent H. V. Gates and Conductor Charles Drennan Kennedy. The two men in the baggage car are Walter Bargess and William Toner. Notice the three-foot iron bar on the pilot used before automatic couplers were invented.

OREGON PACIFIC RAILROAD COMPANY.

TIME TABLE NO. 3,

Taking effect at 7.10 A. M., Monday, June 21st, 1886.

☞ FOR THE GOVERNMENT OF EMPLOYEES ONLY. ◄

EASTWARD.		MILES FROM YAQUINA.	STATIONS.		MILES FROM CORVALLIS.	WESTWARD.	
No. 3.	No. 1.					No. 2.	No. 4.
FREIGHT.	PASSENGER.					PASSENGER.	FREIGHT.
7.50 A. M.	7.10 A. M.		LV. ✗ YAQUINA AR. 5.2		72.0	6.40 P. M.	3.00 P. M.
8.25	7.30	5.2	MILL NO. 4 2 3.8		66.8	6.23	2.25
8.45	7.45	9.0	TOLEDO 3 6.3		63.0	6.10	2.00
9.25	8.15	15.3	SIDING NO. 1 4 8.7		56.7	5.45	1.20
10.15	8.50	24.0	CHITWOOD 5 4.5		48.0	5.13	12.30
10.40	9.08	28.5	LITTLE ELK 6 7.5		43.5	4.55	12.00 NOON
11.25	9.35	36.0	NORTON'S 7 5.0		36.0	4.25	11.15
11.55	9.55	41.0	NASHVILLE 8 5.0		31.0	4.05	10.45
A. 12.25 P. M. D. 1.55	10.15	46.0	✗ SUMMIT 9 10.2		26.0	3.45	D. 10.15 A. 10.05
3.05	10.55	56.2	✗ HARRIS' • 2.5		15.8	3.05	9.05
3.20	11.05	58.7	SIDING NO. 2 11 7.3		13.3	2.55	8.50
4.05	11.35	66.0	PHILOMATH 12 6.0		6.0	2.25	8.05
4.40 P. M.	11.58 A. M.	72.0	AR. ✗ CORVALLIS 13 LV.			2.00 P. M.	7.30 A. M.

Nos. 1 and 2 runs daily except Sunday.   No. 3 runs Mondays and Fridays.   No. 4 runs Tuesdays and Saturdays.

H. V. GATES, SUPERINTENDENT.

The Payroll Train

It's the tenth of the month and pay day! Everyone anticipates the arrival of the payroll train. A company policeman guards the door of the cage with a revolver in his belt and in the cage the paymaster stands behind a counter piled with stacks of silver dollars, fifty-cent pieces, quarters and nickels, which he replenishes from the iron box beside him on the floor. After paying off the men in the shops the train starts "down the line" stopping at every station with wages for the agents, section crews and telegraph operators. The help were usually paid by check but many of the employees would endorse their check and have the cash for immediate payment of their monthly bills.

1890 Payroll Train, Southern Pacific No. 10, a wood burning Baldwin locomotive (4-4-0) westbound, stops in front of the railroad station at Oregon City. The coach being pulled has a cage at one end and a small cooking section at the other end to feed the crew. The men in the white uniforms handle kitchen work.

SP No. 16, the "California Express," taken somewhere in southern Oregon in about 1893. The train is "in the hole" (sidetrack for passing trains) to meet a train coming in the opposite direction. Note the express car at the rear of the train. This was so would-be robbers, after halting the train, would have to march the engineer and fireman past, hopefully alerting passengers to reach the treasure.

1893 SCHEDULE:

| Lv. Portland | SP No. 15 California Express | 7:00 P.M. | Monday |
| Ar. San Francisco | SP No. 15 California Express | 8:15 A.M. | Wednesday |

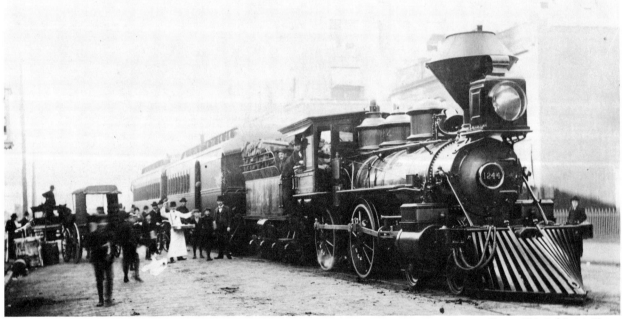

Oregon Historical Society Photo

Southern Pacific train No. 2, the "Corvallis Mail," stopping at Fourth and Stark Streets in downtown Portland in 1895. The train has arrived from Corvallis by way of McMinnville and is pulled by wood burning locomotive No. 1244 (4-4-0). The man in the white apron is the train "News Butcher" who has made the trip from Corvallis selling newspapers, magazines, candies etc.

1895 SCHEDULE:

| Lv. Corvallis | SP No. 2 Corvallis Mail | 12:55 P.M. | Monday |
| Ar. Portland | SP No. 2 Corvallis Mail | 5:30 P.M. | Monday |

The "Suburban Local," one of the many daily suburban trains operating between Jefferson Street Terminal in Portland and Oswego, serving Portland well-to-do people residing in Fulton, Riverdale and what is today called Dunthorpe. Shown is the two-car train pulled by locomotive No. 1510 (4-4-0) and the train crew *(left to right):* Marion Young, brakeman; A. B. "Daisy" Bell, conductor; G. Cundiff, fireman; and Lewis G. Williams, engineer. This photo was taken at Oswego Station in about 1905. The City of Portland recently decided to use the same right of way between Jefferson Street in Portland and Oswego for light rail (street car) service.

An extra freight train, as indicated by the white flag, is pulled by Corvallis & Eastern engine No. 4 (4-4-0 Standard wood burner) into Albany yard in 1910 with Jess Brown at the controls. Note the "shunting bar" hanging under the tender directly below the large number 4. This is an eight-foot wooden bar with heavy iron caps on each end. These caps are designed to nest in the pole socket located on the pilot beam and also at the rear of the tender. The shunting bar is removed from the tender by the brakeman who holds one end against the pole socket of the engine while the other is extended lengthwise toward the boxcar to be moved. If all goes well and the pole is socketed properly, the car on the opposite track will move easily. Mishaps were known to occur frequently, as faulty ground conditions, rainy weather or rocky soil could often result in "curtains" for the brakeman if he lost his footing. This practice, quite general at one time, was outlawed a few years back.

Above, SP No. 13, the "San Francisco Express," taken somewhere in southern Oregon pulled by a double-header (two
locomotives) necessary for the steep grades over the Siskiyou
Mountains.

1910 SCHEDULE:

Lv. Portland	SP No. 13 San Francisco Express	1:30 A.M.	Monday
Ar. San Francisco	SP No. 13 San Francisco Express	12:28 P.M.	Tuesday

"The Tillamook Local," 1911

Above and below, installing and repairing the electrified overhead wire along with ground poles to hold the hot wire, taken somewhere along the West Side Line in about 1912 or 1913.

The Red Electrics

The Southern Pacific electrified its presently in use West Side branch line, originally built under the names "Oregon Central Railroad" and later the "Western Oregon Railroad." Historians have mixed opinions as to why SP spent millions of dollars electrifying its line considering that a service was already available with steam trains. Some will tell you it was a grudge fight between Edward Henry Harriman, who controlled the SP, and James Jerome Hill, The Empire Builder, who was the boss of the Northern Pacific-Great Northern-Burlington combination. Some say Harriman built the electric line to keep Hill and his Oregon Electric line from controlling the Willamette Valley.

Others feel Hill built the Oregon Electric to keep Harriman from expanding. It is not even certain who had the electrification idea first.

Regardless of who did what, the fact remains that there was tremendous growth in the Oregon Country and improvements in transportation were needed. Portland was advertising in national magazines that it would be a city of five hundred thousand people by 1912.

The "Red Electrics" were distinguished by their bright red color. They drew their power from an overhead electric wire. They were built by the Pullman Company of Chicago and serviced the Willamette Valley

The crew of the first Southern Pacific "Red Electric" which rolled on February 17, 1914, and carried 275 passengers in six cars from Portland to Whiteson and back stopping at every important station along the way. *Left to right:* A. L. Lucas, engineer; Mr. Meyers, Pullman Company electrician; E. A. Culp, brakeman; J. T. Clow, conductor; and J. D. Jackson, brakeman.

An end view of a "Red Electric"; photo number 1

An end view of a "Red Electric"; photo number 2

for a comparatively short time. They were yet another step in the evolution of railroading.

On January 18, 1914, the first "Red Electric" ran from Portland to Whiteson in Yamhill County, a distance of forty-five miles. The electrification program was extended to Corvallis in Benton County in 1917, making a total distance of 87.8 miles of electrified line. The public accepted these new red painted cars as a new innovation in the transportation field, but by the 1930s the automobile, with its independent mobility on our fine highway system, had brought nearly all types of electric short-line and interurban service to its knees.

On this and the following two pages are photos of the "Red Electric" from various views. The photos are numbered and a de-

scription of each follows.

Photo number 1 is an end view of a Passenger Control Trailer without a pantograph. The two upright cylinders on the deck of the flooring, called grab irons, were the only protection for patrons walking between cars while the train was in motion. The round windows were a safety feature to motormen in the event of an accident. Previous similar equipment had large rectangular windows. The small, round cupler socket directly in front of the air gong is opening for the train cable coupler, an electrical tube sometimes called a "stinger," extending the full length of the car and placed on the roof of cars for safety reasons.

Photo number 2 is a Passenger Motor car with a raised overhead pantograph. The cupler socket is opened and the train cable

An end view of a "Red Electric"; photo number 3

An end view of a "Red Electric"; photo number 4

coupler is plugged in ready to use on a connecting car. Note the safety lights on the roof. These may have been used at some time but generally kerosene markers were hung individually on the metal clamps seen on each corner of the car.

Photos number 3 and 4 are head-end cars (no front doors). Photo 3 is a Baggage Passenger car while photo 4 is a Baggage Express car with a pantograph. The metal ladder shown on each end of the cars is for employees only. Note that neither car has a headlight for night use. Lights were installed manually by motormen at the beginning and end of each trip.

Photos 5 and 6 are side views of the "Red Electric" with raised pantographs. Photo 5 is of a Coach Motor car and has sixty passenger seats. Photo 6 is of a Combination car (baggage/passenger) and has fifty-two passenger seats. Notice that the cars each have a ladder on the baggage end for employees and that both cars have a box-like frame raising the pantograph above the roof of the car. These were installed by Southern Pacific after the cars were received from the Pullman Company to give more pressure against the hot wire.

Photos 7 and 8 are outside and inside views, respectively, of a Box Motor (baggage express) car. In photo 8, note the flooring which runs in an opposite direction in the lower left-hand corner. This spot is reserved for ice or lading with a leaking water content.

Photos 9 and 10 are inside views of passenger coaches. Photo 9 is a Baggage Passenger car with a smoker section and has fifty-two seats. Photo 10 is a sixty-seat Coach Motor car.

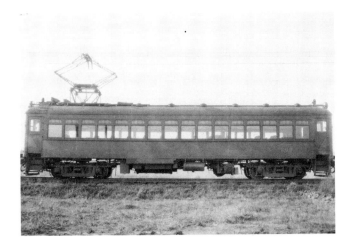

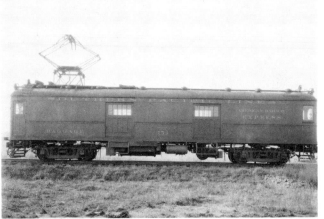

Above, a side view of a "Red Electric"; photo number 5

Above, a side view of a "Red Electric"; photo number 6

A side view of a "Red Electric" baggage express; photo number 7

An inside view of a "Red Electric" baggage express; photo number 8

An inside view of a "Red Electric" passenger car; photo number 9

An inside view of a "Red Electric" passenger car; photo number 10

Above, two-car "Red Electrics" near Newberg, Oregon

Right, along the line

A "Red Electric" train on Fourth Avenue in downtown Portland. This is the original Oregon Central track used before the turn of the century. Note that the first half of the train can be seen two or three blocks ahead. The city of Portland passed an ordinance that no more than three cars could operate as one train on the city streets of Portland. This necessitated the SP keeping an extra engineer always available for when a train had to be divided.

THE COMPLETION of Elk Rock Tunnel on the Southern Pacific, East Side Electric Line, between Portland and Oswego was celebrated Monday morning, December 5, 1921.

Now that the movement of trains across Elk Rock Trestle is a matter of history, a few facts and figures relating to this improvement should be of interest.

The entire cost of Elk Rock Tunnel approximates $350,000.

It is more than a quarter of a mile long. The actual measurements are length 1395 feet, height 23½ feet, width 18 feet.

IN PENETRATING Elk Rock it was necessary to remove nearly 31,000 cubic yards of decomposed basalt, of which the cliff is chiefly composed at a depth of 100 to 150 feet behind the face.

The portals of the tunnel are lined with concrete for a depth of 50 feet, the remainder being timber lined with Port Orford cedar.

The track within the tunnel is on a double reverse curve and along the sides are electric lights.

During the construction period June 1 to December 5, an average of 100 men were employed. The work was carried on day and night—twenty-four hours a day.

Tunnel and Trestle at Elk Rock

THE ORIGINAL Elk Rock Trestle 1050 feet in length was constructed and placed in service during the winter of 1887.

At that time it was considered quite an engineering feat.

The building of the trestle furnished the missing link in the Willamette Valley Railway, a narrow gauge line extending south to Dundee, which was built in 1885-6 by Mr. Dundee Reid, and associates.

In 1893 this line was taken over by the Oregon and California R. R. Company. Shortly after the track was widened to standard gauge, and the trestle reconstructed.

PRIOR To the construction of the trestle in the latter part of 1887, through service to Portland was maintained for about a year and a half by the use of a steamboat.

This steamboat operated from the foot of Jefferson Street in Portland to a point on the shore of the Willamette River, at the south end of Elk Rock Trestle.

Only a few years ago, a portion of the old boatslip near Elk Rock Trestle was still in evidence, as mute testimony to the progress of transportation.

This is from a promotional brochure announcing the completion of the Elk Rock Tunnel, issued by the Southern Pacific in 1921.

Right, the first "Red Electric" train through Elk Rock Tunnel with Engineer William F. "Billie" Schellenberg at the controls.

Train tracks built near the water

A "Red Electric" connects with SP No. 379, the "Willamina Local," at Whiteson pulled by engine No. 1358 (4-4-0). Fireman W. C. Haffner is in the gangway.

1922 SCHEDULE:

Lv. Portland	SP No. 353 Red Electrics	4:30 P.M.	Monday
Ar. Whiteson	SP No. 353 Red Electrics	6:30 P.M.	Monday
Lv. Whiteson	SP No. 379 Willamina Local	6:35 P.M.	Monday
Ar. Willamina	SP No. 379 Willamina Local	7:30 P.M.	Monday

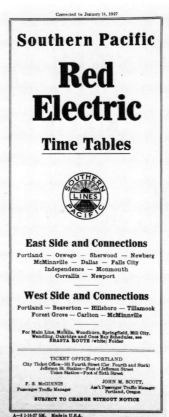

Corrected to January 14, 1927

Southern Pacific
Red Electric
Time Tables

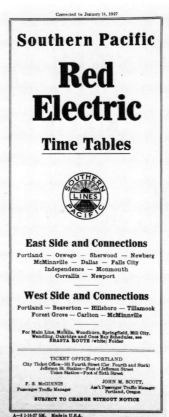

East Side and Connections

Portland — Oswego — Sherwood — Newberg
McMinnville — Dallas — Falls City
Independence — Monmouth
Corvallis — Newport

West Side and Connections

Portland — Beaverton — Hillsboro — Tillamook
Forest Grove — Carlton — McMinnville

For Main Line, Molalla, Woodburn, Springfield, Mill City,
Wendling, Oakridge and Coos Bay Schedules, see
SHASTA ROUTE (white) Folder

TICKET OFFICE—PORTLAND
City Ticket Office—101 Fourth Street (Cor. Fourth and Stark)
Jefferson St. Station—Foot of Jefferson Street
Union Station—Foot of Sixth Street

F. S. McGINNIS   JOHN M. SCOTT,
Passenger Traffic Manager   Ass't Passenger Traffic Manager
                                         Portland, Oregon

SUBJECT TO CHANGE WITHOUT NOTICE

A—3 1-14-27 5M. Made in U.S.A.

SOUTHERN PACIFIC RED ELECTRICS — FROM PORTLAND to Oswego, Lake Grove and Tualatin

Stations	M.	†303	*305	*351	*357	*309	*359	*311	*313	*353	*315	†355	*317	‡ Special	*319	*323	
Lv PORTLAND, Un. Sta.	.0		7 15	8.00	9.45	12.15	1.15		3.35	4.30		5.40		6.45			
Ankeny Street	.5	6.43	7.18					1.55			5.08		6.25		8 00	11.25	
4TH & STARK ST. (Tkt. Ofc.).	.8	6.45	7.20	8.05	9.50	12.20	1.20	1.57	3.40	4.35	5.10	5.45	6.27	6.50	8.02	11.27	
Fourth and Jefferson	1.1	f 6 48	f 7 23	f 8 08	f 9 53	f12.23	f 1.23	f 2.00	f 3.43	f 4.38	f 5.13	f 5.48	f 6.30	f	8.05	f11.30	
Lv Jefferson St. (Station)	1.4	f 6 52	7.26	8.12	9.56	12.27	1.26	2.05	3.46	4.43	5.16	5.51	f 6.33		8.08	f11.33	
Turntable	2.1	f 6 55	f 7 28			f12.29		f 2.05	f 3.48		f 5.18		f 6.35		f 8.10	f11.35	
Mulbox	2.9	f 6 57	f 7 29			f12.30		f 2.06	f 3.50		f 5.20	f 6.53	f 6.36		f 8.11	f11.36	
Zimmerman	3.1	f 6 58	f 7 30			f12.31		f 2.07	f 3.51		f 5.21		f 6.37		f 8.12	f11.37	
Jones	3.5	f															
Southern Portland	3.9	f 7 01	f 7 32		f10.02	f12.33		f 2.09	f 3.53		f 5.23		f 6.39		f 8.14	f11.39	
Fulton	4.3	f 7 02	f 7 33		f10.03	f12.34		f 2.10	f 3.54		f 5.24		f 6.40		f 8.15	f11.40	
Cemetery	4.7	f 7 05	f 7 34		f10.05	f12.35		f 2.11	f 3.55		f 5.26	f 5.58	f 6.41		f 8.16	f11.41	
Ewahwe	4.9	f 7 07	f 7 36		f10.07	f12.37		f 2.13	f 3.57		f 5.28	f 6.00	f 6.43		f 8.18	f11.43	
Riverdale	6.1	f 7 08	f 7 37		f10.08	f12.38		f 2.14	f 3.58		f 5.29	f 6.01	f 6.44		f 8.19	f11.44	
Rivera	6.3	f 7 09	f 7 38		f10.09	f12.39		f 2.15	f 3.59		f 5.30	f 6.02	f 6.45		f 8.20	f11.45	
Riverwood	6 6	f															
Elk Rock	6.8	f 7 10	f 7 39		f10.10	f12.40		f 2.16	f 4.00		f 5.31		f 6.46		f 8.21	f11.46	
Rock Spur	7.4	f 7 13	f 7 40		f10.11	f12.42		f 2.17	f 4.01		f 5.32	f 6.05	f 6.47		f 8.22	f11.47	
Briarwood	7.6	f															
Wilsonia	8.1	f 7 15	f 7 41		f10.13	f12.44		f 2.19	f 4.03		f 5.34	f 6.08	f 6.49		f 8.24	f11.49	
Ar OSWEGO	8.4	7.17	7 45	8.30	10.15	12.45	1.45	2.21	4.05	4.59	5.36	6.10	6.51	7.12	8.26	11.51	
Goodin	10.8	f											f		f 8.33	f11.57	
Lake Grove	11.0	f 7 23		f 8.38	f10.21	12.53	f 1.52	f 2.28	f 4 11	5.05	f 5.43	f 6.18	f 6.58	f	8.34	f11.58	
Bryant	11.7	f 7 24	f 7 53	f 8.39	f10 22	12.54	f 1.53	f 2.29	f 4 12	5.06	f 5.44	f 6.19	f 6.59	7.20	8.35	f11.59	
Cook	12.2	7.25	7.55	8 40	10 24	12.55	1.55	2 30	4.13	5.08	5.45	6.21	7.00				
Jean	12.7	f			f	f						f					
Galbraith	13 8	f			f	f						f					
Ar TUALATIN	14.2			8 44	10.28		1.59			5.12		6.25		7.25			

*Daily.   †Daily except Sunday.   (f)Flag.   All outbound trains stop at Morrison Street.   ‡Sunday Only.

Corrected to June 1, 1925
Light face type A. M.   Black face type P. M.
Subject to change without notice

Southern Pacific Red Electrics — TO PORTLAND from Forest Grove, Hillsboro and Beaverton

CORRECTED TO JUNE 1, 1925
Light Face A.M.   Dark Face P.M.
Subject to Change Without Notice

Stations	Miles	†120	†134	*126	*124‡	*128‡	†130	†122	Sun. Only	*136	
Lv.FOREST GROVE Tkt. Office	.0		6.05	6.50	8.41	12.25	3.30	5.15	6.15		
Eddy (Masonic Home)	1.3		f	f	f	f	f	f	f		
Catching	1.8		f 6.08	f 6.53	f 8.45	f12.29	f 3.33	f 5.18	f 6.18		
Cornelius	2.7		6.10	6 55	8.48	12.32	3.35	5.20	6.20		
Killgore	3.7		f	f	f	f	f	f	f		
Jobe	4.6		f 6.13	f 6.58	f 8.51	f12.35	f 3.38	f 5.23	f 6.23		
Hillsboro, Ticket Office	6.8		6.20	7.05	9.04	12.46	3.44	5.31	6.31	10.30	
Newton	8.8		f 6.25	f 7.10	f 9.09	f12.51	f 3.51	f 5.36	f 6.36	f10.35	
Matson	9.8	Dly Ex San	f 6.27	f 7.12	f 9.11	f12.53	f 3.53	f 5.38	f 6.38	f10.37	
Hays	10.2		f	f	f	f	f	f	f	f	
Witch Hazel	10.5		f 6.28	f 7.13	f 9.12	f12.54	f 3.54	f 5.39	f 6.39	f10.38	
Reedville	11.9	5.55	f 6.31	f 7.16	f 9.15	12.57	3.57	5.42	6.42	10.40	
Tobias	12.6		f	f	f	f	f	f	f	f	
Aloha	13.4	f 5.58	f 6.35	7 20	9.17	1.00	f 4.00	f 5.45	f 6.45	f10.42	
Huber	14.0	f 6.00	f 6.38	7.22	9.19	1.01	f 4.02	f 5.47	f 6.47	f10.43	
St. Mary's	15.1	f 6.02	f 6.40	f 7 24	9.21	f 1.03	f 4.05	f 5.49	f 6.49	f10.45	
Beaverton	16.4	6.06	6.45	7.29	9.26	1.06	4.10	5.54	6.54	10.48	
Arrow	17.3	f			f	f	f	f	f	f	
Raleigh	18.5	f 6.10	f 6.49	7 35	f 9.31	1.10	4.15	5.58	6.58	10.52	
Olsen	19.5	f 6.12	f 6.51	f 7 37	f 9.32	f 1.12	f 4.20	f 6.00	f 7.00	f10.54	
Shattuck	19.8	f 6.13	f 6.53	f 7.38	f 9.34	f 1.13	f 4.21	f 6.01	f 7.01	f10.55	
Woodrow	20.4	f			f	f	f	f	f	f	
Pine	20.9	f			f	f	f	f	f	f	
Dosch	21.4	f 6.15	f 6.56	f 7 40	f 9.35	f 1.16	f 4.23	f 6.03	f 7.03	f10.57	
Bertha	21.9		6 20	7.01	7.45	9.41	1.19	4.28	6.07	7.07	10.59
Third and Miles Streets	23.1	f 6 22	f 7.03	f 7 50	f 9.45	s	f 4.30	f 6.12	f 7.12	f11 01	
Bancroft	24.7	f 6 26	f 7.09	f 7 53	f 9.49	f 1.26	f 4.35	f 6.16	f 7.16	f11.04	
Fourth and Jefferson	26.3	f 6 34	7.18	8.01	9.58	1.34	4.43	6.26	7.26	11.11	
4TH & STARK ST. (Tkt. Office)	26 5	6.38	7 23	8 08	10.03	1.39	4.47	6.32	7.32	11.15	
Ar. PORTLAND Union Station	27.4		7.30	8 15	10.10	1.45	4.55	6.40	7.40		

(f) Flag Stop. Trains stop at Salmon, Morrison, Burnside and Flanders Streets, Portland, and flag at 3rd and 5th Sts. and 3rd Ave. Forest Grove; N. Range and Fir, N. Range and Main, 6th and Main, 6th and Fir, 10th St., Hillsboro; Ware; Hays; Hefter; Archer; Hooker St., Portland, Mile Post 779.9 between Woodrow and Dosch. All trains inbound stop 4th and College Sts. except 122 and 124 stop on flag. *Daily.

†Connects with Tillamook Branch train at N. Range and Main Street Hillsboro

Another Money Saver!

the **Red Electric**

ONE DAY ROUND TRIP TICKET

**A new ticket on sale daily that
entitles you to make the round
trip to any Red Electric station
Portland to Amity inclusive
at the regular**

One Way Fare
Plus One Tenth

Note these examples:

From ☞ To	Huber	Aloha	Reedville
Forest Grove	.60	.55	.50
Hillsboro	.30	.30	.25
McMinnville	1.55	1.50	1.45
Portland	.55	.60	.65
Yamhill	1.10	1.10	1.05

**Return portion of ticket will be honored
on any train leaving prior to midnight
on day of purchase**

**The popular 10-Ride ticket continues
on sale--good for one or more
traveling together and
for sixty days**

Southern Pacific

S. E. ANZALONE, Agt., Huber   J. H. BUCK, Agt., Aloha   E. J. LOWRY, Agt., Reedville

a-43   5-25-27   1M

This photo, taken near Sherwood, Oregon in the 1930s, shows railroad electricians removing the overhead hot wire used by the "Red Electrics." At the rear of the train is Conductor E. A. Culp. SP No. 354, the "McMinnville Local," was the last "Red Electric" train operated on October 5, 1929 with Conductor Le Baron Hendricks in charge.

Inside and outside views of a freight electric engine, Portland Eugene & Eastern No. 100, a sixty-ton locomotive.

This gas electric "Motor Coach" was purchased from the Pullman Company in 1930 to be used over the same route the "Red Electrics" had used before being discontinued in 1929. The railroad expected to continue with the U.S. Mail contract and hoped to operate as interurban service. It only continued about one year or so.

1931 SCHEDULE:

Lv. Portland	SP No. 351 Motor Coach	7:30 A.M.	Monday
Ar. Corvallis	SP No. 351 Motor Coach	10:55 A.M.	Monday
Lv. Corvallis	SP No. 352 Motor Coach	1:40 P.M.	Monday
Ar. Portland	SP No. 352 Motor Coach	5:05 P.M.	Monday

A 1915 view of SP train No. 11, the "Shasta Limited," with the engine force in front of locomotive No. 2348 (4-6-0 Baldwin) and taken shortly before the train left Portland. The "Shasta" name has been around for a long time. It was used shortly after the Oregon & California Railroad became a part of the Southern Pacific lines. Train numbers were changed frequently but the name continued.

Shasta Limited

Extra Fare $5.00

from

Seattle, Tacoma and Portland to San Francisco Daily

Leaves Seattle	- -	9:30 A. M.
Tacoma	- -	10:50 A. M.
Portland	- -	3:50 P. M.
Arrives San Francisco	-	6:50 P. M.

A daily train with every convenience for travelers, including Barber Shop, Shower Bath, Valet Service, Ladies' Maid, Manicuring, Hairdressing, Stenographer, Stock and News Reports.

Clubroom-Observation Car, containing Ladies' Parlor and Library, Standard Pullman Drawing Room Sleeping Cars, Compartment Cars and unexcelled Dining Car service.

PROTECTED BY AUTOMATIC ELECTRIC BLOCK SAFETY SIGNALS

(Oct 1915)

The "Shasta Limited" around 1925

The Shasta Limited

In 1913 the first through Pullman cars were operated from Portland to Los Angeles using No. 11, the "Shasta Limited," to Oakland and No. 76, the "Lark," to Los Angeles. This continued until about 1927 when the first through train, SP No. 15-60, the "Southern California Express," was started. This name was changed to the "West Coast Limited" in about 1928. Train No. 15-60 was a through train but changed train numbers at Sacramento.

All trains going towards Sacramento or San Francisco (No. 15) were going railroad westbound. All trains going away from Sacramento or San Francisco (No. 60) were going railroad eastbound. This accounts for odd-number trains into Sacramento and even-numbered trains out of Sacramento.

Southern Pacific train No. 19, the "Cottage Grove Local," in 1915 entering Oregon City at Singer Hill Crossing pulled by locomotive No. 3071 (4-4-2). Note the flagman on duty.

1915 SCHEDULE:

Lv. Portland	SP No. 19 Cottage Grove Local	2:00 P.M.	Monday
Ar. Oregon City	SP No. 19 Cottage Grove Local	2:43 P.M.	Monday
Ar. Cottage Grove	SP No. 19 Cottage Grove Local	7:40 P.M.	Monday

SP No. 53, the "Exposition Special," was started in 1915 because of heavy traffic to the Panama-Pacific International Exposition in San Francisco. The train was so popular it was continued for several years afterwards as the "Golden Gate Special."

Golden Gate Special
— TO —

California

Lv. Portland 8.30 A.M.
instead of 12.40 P.M.
Ar. San Francisco 5.30 P.M.

New Train to California April 30th.

Excellent service provided from Pacific Northwest points to California. Good connection made at Portland and San Francisco. Saves 12 hours time to Southern California.

Complete information can be obtained
from local agent.
(May 1916)

Coach car of the early 1920s

New
Limited Train

to

Willamette Valley Points

on following schedule:

8.00 A.M.	Lv.	Portland	Av.	5.00 P.M.
8.45 A.M.		Oregon City		4.10 P.M.
9.25 A.M.		Woodburn		3.33 P.M.
10.01 A.M.		Salem		3.02 P.M.
10.46 A.M.		Albany		2.16 P.M.
11.38 A.M.		Junction City		1.25 P.M.
12.01 P.M.	Av.	Eugene	Lv.	1.00 P.M.

Connection arrives Corvallis 11.30 A.M.
Connection leaves Corvallis 1.30 P.M.

Excellent service provided
between all commercial
centers of the Willamette
Valley. All steel cars,
rock ballasted roadbed and
fast time enroute are
features of

Southern Pacific Service
(May 1916)

Southern Pacific service time schedule to Willamette Valley points

SP train No. 23, the "Coos Bay Limited," in 1917

Program

NORTH BEND DAY
August 24th

Band Concerts — Speaking Ceremonies — Dedication Simpson Park
Street Carnival — Water Sports — Parades — Driving Goldenspike.

COOS COUNTY DAY
August 25th

Trips by rail and boat to Coquille, Bandon, Myrtle Point, Powers,
Coos Bay, Mussel Reef, Sunset Bay, Cape Arago. Sea food dinner
at Charleston Bay. Fishing at Lakeside—Launch trips on Coos Bay.

MARSHFIELD DAY
August 26th

Industrial Parade—Water Sports—Auto Racing—Illuminated Launch
Parade — Fireworks — Dancing — Horse Racing.

SPECIAL TRAINS FROM

Portland   Salem   Eugene   San Francisco

Low Round Trip Fares, on sale August 21 to 26 inc.
Return Limit August 31

CITY TICKET OFFICE: Corner Sixth and Oak Streets, or East
Morrison or Union Stations.

JOHN M. SCOTT, Gen. Pass. Agt.
Portland, Oregon

 SOUTHERN PACIFIC
(1916)

1916 celebration for the coming of the railroad to the Coos Bay country.

"The Oregonian" — Portland to San Francisco. This train operated during
World War I and continued until the close of World War II. Train numbers
and schedules were changed many times.

1930 SCHEDULE:

Lv. Portland	SP No. 17 The Oregonian	9:50 P.M.	Monday
Ar. San Francisco	SP No. 17 The Oregonian	6:52 P.M.	Tuesday

COMPLETELY AIR-CONDITIONED

Every car on our popular West Coast, between Portland and Los Angeles, is completely air-conditioned—modern reclining chair cars, improved tourist Pullmans, dining car and observation car. Passengers enjoy the cool, clean comfort which only air-conditioning can give, regardless of the accommodations they choose.

This popular Shasta Route train gives through service daily between Portland and Los Angeles. It leaves Portland nightly at 10:15 and arrives Los Angeles at 8:50 the second morning. Convenient connection is provided at Los Angeles with our famous Sunset Limited and at Portland with trains to the north and east. The schedule:

SOUTHBOUND	NORTHBOUND
Lv. Portland......10:15 p.m.	Lv. Los Angeles 7:45 p.m.
Ar. Los Angeles 8:50 a.m.	Ar. Portland.......7:30 a.m.

The West Coast speeds over the Cascade line of the Shasta Route and through the broad, fertile Sacramento and San Joaquin valleys, giving a trip of unusual scenic interest.

In addition to the special plate meals on the West Coast dining car, you also have your choice of our famous "Meals Select"—complete breakfasts as low as 50c and full-course luncheons and dinners for as little as 80c. In coaches and tourist sleeping cars we serve coffee, sandwiches, fruit, ice cream, pastries and similar items for 5c and 10c.

Printed in U. S. A.

A Typical Menu:

Chilled Grape Fruit

or

Dry or Cooked Cereal with Cream

Roll with Butter or Toast

Coffee   Tea   Milk

A time schedule and advertisement for SP No. 15-60, the "West Coast Limited," a through train from Portland to Los Angeles in 1928. Note the charges for eating in the dining car and prices available during the depression years of the early 1930s.

The interior of the Portland Bus Depot in about 1930. The benches were formerly used by railroad patrons at the Union Station.

The Oregon Auto Stage Terminal at Park and Yamhill Streets in Portland. The 1916 Cadillac and 1916 White, two busses of the Portland Stage Line, are loading passengers for Salem.

Southern Pacific in the Bus Business

During the last few years of the 1920s and the early 1930s the Southern Pacific Railroad Company entered the bus business. The many new highways built by the State were something new and interesting to the general public. They were yet another step in the evolution of transportation.

Little by little the "Red Electrics" were removed in favor of the automobile/bus sub-stitution. The private automobile was a growing problem for any type of public transportation during this period. SP even began operating bus traffic in competition with its own deluxe trains to California. Eventually this traffic was taken over by Greyhound Lines in which the SP had a strong financial, but not an operating, interest for many years.

A Southern Pacific stage ready to leave the Salmon Street Stage Terminal in Portland for California in about 1929. Joseph W. Gaines (*inside the bus*) is shaking hands with one of his friends.

Lounge car on the "New Cascade Limited." The "Cascade Limited" became the deluxe extra fare train in 1928, an honor that had been given to the "Shasta" for many years. Its train number has changed several times, from No. 17 in 1928, to No. 23 in 1937 and to No. 11 in 1947. It was always a money-making train, due to the consistent traffic to California.

1933 SCHEDULE:

Lv. San Francisco	SP No. 18 Cascade Limited	6:20 P.M.	Monday
Ar. Klamath Falls	SP No. 18 Cascade Limited	6:20 A.M.	Tuesday
Ar. Eugene	SP No. 18 Cascade Limited	12:13 P.M.	Tuesday
Ar. Portland	SP No. 18 Cascade Limited	3:55 P.M.	Tuesday

SP No. 18, the "Cascade Limited," winding around beautiful Odell Lake. An open top observation car was added to this train at Klamath Falls and removed at Eugene so patrons could enjoy the green mountain areas of Oregon.

1937 Schedule:

Lv. Portland	SP No. 23 Cascade Limited	5:40 P.M.	Monday
Ar. San Francisco	SP No. 23 Cascade Limited	1:32 P.M.	Tuesday

SP No. 23, the "Cascade Limited," passing Westmoreland Golf Course on the edge of Portland pulled by locomotive No. 4364 (4-8-2)

A private room car on the "New Cascade"

"ALL ABOARD," Conductor Ernest Therron "Buck" Morian calls shortly before the departure of the "Cascade."

Inside the "New Cascade"

SP No. 19, the "Klamath Limited," westbound near Woodburn, Oregon, pulled by a 4400 class locomotive (4-8-4). The train name "Klamath Limited" has been in use since 1929 on various schedules for trains operating through Klamath Falls, Oregon.

1943 SCHEDULE:

Lv. Portland	SP No. 19 Klamath	8:00 A.M.	Monday
Ar. San Francisco	SP No. 19 Klamath	10:45 A.M.	Tuesday

Left, inside the dining room of the "Klamath"

Below, a vintage coach of the day

RPO — Railroad Post Office — It was a great day when the railroads handled the U.S. Mail. This photo shows the interior of a railroad-owned but government-operated traveling post office. The mail was distributed to all of the various towns along the line and was handled with the same speed that the first-class passengers enjoyed.

At the last moment U.S. Mail could be deposited into the mail car directly. It was cancelled with RPO cancellation by mailman handling.

"Children's Day Special" at the Oregon State Fair in 1935. A special train was operated for the Portland Oregon Journal Juniors. Train stops were made along the way for children from small towns and farming areas to enjoy the fun. The above photo was taken in front of the railroad station at Fair Grounds, the entrance to the Oregon State Fair in Salem.

CHILDREN'S DAY
OREGON STATE FAIR
Sat., Sept. 28th

Round Trip Tickets at Low Cost Including Admission to the Fair

	School Children		Adults
	14 years and under	over 14 years	
Oregon City	$0.75	$1.00	$1.25
Canby Aurora	.55	.85	1.10
Hubbard	.45	.70	.95
Woodburn Gervais Brooks	.30	.55	.80

GOOD ONLY ON SPECIAL TRAIN

Leaving OREGON CITY	-	9.49 a. m.
CANBY	-	f10.06
BARLOW	-	f
AURORA	-	f10.11
HUBBARD	-	f10.18
WOODBURN	-	10.25
GERVAIS	-	f10.32
BROOKS	-	f10.39
Arriving FAIR GROUNDS	-	10.50 a. m.

RETURNING

Leaving FAIR GROUNDS   -   5.30 p. m

Go—See the wonderful displays of Oregon Products, Live Stock, and the many other exhibits of intense interest. Special Children's Day Program has been especially arranged by the State Fair Board.

Please buy your tickets in advance to avoid congestion at train time.

SOUTHERN PACIFIC

Southern Pacific freight train No. 663, the "Seagull," westbound between Portland and Salem en route to California in 1940. The train is pulled by SP engine No. 5005, a 4-10-2 Schenectady, built in 1925. When SP No. 5005 was first built it was the most powerful freight engine in the world.

Left, an engineer at work inside the "Seagull"

Right, inside the little red caboose of a freight train with Conductor Clarence Edmund Sandefer *(left)* and Brakeman Henry William Friesen *(right)*.

1941 Schedule:

Lv. Portland	SP No. 11 Beaver	5:20 P.M.	Monday
Ar. San Francisco	SP No. 11 Beaver	1:00 P.M.	Tuesday

FOR CHAIR CAR AND TOURIST PASSENGERS ONLY

FOR TRAIN COMFORT at the lowest possible cost try the friendly *Beaver*. It's really fun to save money on this popular chair car and tourist train which speeds daily to and from San Francisco.

CHAIR SP 2431

FREE PILLOWS, porter service, air conditioning, spacious rest rooms, add to the comfort of riding in these luxurious chair cars.

TWO STREAMLINED chair cars on the *Beaver* have new-type reclining and adjustable chairs cushioned with foam rubber; extra wide windows.

These are typical Beaver Menus, changed daily.

BREAKFAST
35c

Tomato Juice

Dry or Cooked Cereal
with Cream

Toast or Muffins

Coffee (Cup)

Milk

Tea (Pot)

LUNCHEON
40c

Potted Breast of Lamb
with Vegetables

Garden Peas   Mashed Potato

Bread and Butter

Ice Cream with Cake

Coffee (Cup)

Milk

Tea (Pot)

DINNER
50c

Filet of Fresh Fish, Remoulade
or
Chicken Pot Pie, Family Style

String Beans   Hashed Browned Potatoes

Dinner Roll

Peach Cobbler, Vanilla Sauce

Coffee (Cup)   Milk   Tea Pot

IN A DOWNY BERTH on the *Beaver's* fine tourist Pullmans you can enjoy a good night's sleep for very little money.

Every regular car on the Beaver is air conditioned.

LOUNGE CAR for tourist car passengers on the *Beaver* is full-length, has comfortable chairs, sofas, magazines, radio and a bar.

35c BUYS a good breakfast on the *Beaver*. Luncheon is only 40c and dinner 50c. Prices for more elaborate meals are proportionately low.

The "Beaver" started operating in 1941 and was an economy or challenger-type of train handling Tourist Pullman and individual reserve chair cars. Economy meals in the diner were a special feature of the train. It was discontinued in 1948 when most western rail lines at that time removed all Tourist Pullman service.

Southern Pacific trains No. 9 and No. 10, the "Shasta Daylight," are pulled by diesel locomotive No. 6003 in July 1949. The "Shasta Daylight" had the fastest passenger schedule ever operated between Portland and San Francisco.

A conductor picks up tickets on the "Shasta Daylight"

Right, the lounge car on the "Shasta Daylight." Notice the upstairs view seats.

Left, "Shasta Daylight" memorabilia

WHEN certain air line promotional efforts took a direct crack at the railroads, SP snapped right back with highly effective rebuttal.

Speedy Schedule

— of —

$15 Special Coach Train

Sundays, Tuesdays and Fridays

Lv. PORTLAND, Union Station.........	10:00 A.M.
" East Morrison St. Sta.	10:08 A.M.
Oregon City	f 10:39 A.M.
Canby	f 10:54 A.M.
Woodburn	f 11:15 A.M.
Salem	11:43 A.M.
Turner	f 11:57 A.M.
Marion	f 12:05 P.M.
Jefferson	f 12:11 P.M.
Albany	12:26 P.M.
Shedd	f 12:40 P.M.
Halsey	f 12:47 P.M.
Harrisburg	f 12:57 P.M.
Junction City	f 1:05 P.M.
Eugene	1:50 P.M.
Springfield	f 2:01 P.M.
Westfir	f 2:55 P.M.
Oakridge	f 3:09 P.M.
McCredie Springs	f 3:33 P.M.
Crescent Lake	5:55 P.M.
Klamath Falls	8:25 P.M.
Davis, Cal.	7:20 A.M.
Sacramento*	9:10 A.M.
Ar. OAKLAND, 16th St................	9:45 A.M.
Ar. SAN FRANCISCO	10:30 A.M.

*Leave Davis 8:47 a.m.

Similar service to Portland from San Francisco 3:00 p. m. Monday, Wednesday and Saturday, arriving Portland 3:30 p. m. day following. $15 one way, or buy round-trip ticket, $30, and return any day (in coaches only) within 15 days.

Southern Pacific

A-95 8-24-27 5M
Printed in U. S. A.

JOHN M. SCOTT,
Asst. Passenger Traffic Manager
Portland, Oregon

Effective May 21, 1928

"Silver-Gray" Motor Coaches

to and from

Eugene, Oregon

Southern Pacific
Motor Transport Company
"The Responsible Way"

A.—5-14-28   Subject to change without notice.

"Silver-Grays" leave and arrive at New Salem Hotel
High Street, between State and Ferry

TO PORTLAND

MOTOR COACHES	A.M.	A.M.	A.M.	P.M.	P.M.	P.M.	P.M.	P.M.	P.M.
Lv. Salem................	7.30	8.30	10.35	12.40	1.35	2.25	4.30	5.30	7.45
Ar. Portland............	9.27	10.28	12.40	2.45	3.40	4.28	6.35	7.35	9.50
TRAINS	A.M.	A.M.	P.M.	P.M.	P.M.	P.M.			
Lv. Salem...............	5.25	6.40	*2.29	4.55	6.05	*8.19	....	....	....
Ar. Portland...........	7.30	8.30	4.15	7.10	8.15	10.15	....	....	....

FROM PORTLAND

MOTOR COACHES	A.M.	A.M.	A.M.	A.M.	P.M.	P.M.	P.M.	P.M.	P.M.
Lv. Portland...........	7.30	8.30	9.30	10.30	1.30	2.30	4.30	5.30	7.30
Ar. Salem..............	9.35	10.35	11.35	12.35	3.35	4.35	6.35	7.35	9.35
TRAINS	A.M.	A.M.	P.M.	P.M.	P.M.	P.M.			
Lv. Portland...........	1.00	8.30	10.00	5.00	9.30	*10.15			
Ar. Salem..............	3.10	10.13	11.43	6.55	11.25	11.54			

TO THE SOUTH

MOTOR COACHES	A.M.	A.M.	A.M.	P.M.	P.M.	P.M.	P.M.
Lv. Salem...............	9.40	10.40	11.40	3.40	4.40	6.37	7.40
Ar. Corvallis..........	11.10	12.28	1.05	....	6.07	8.05	9.10
Ar. Eugene.............	12.40	1.55	....	6.15	7.40	....	10.40
Ar. Roseburg...........	—	4.57	....	9.20			
Ar. Ashland............		10.10	....				
TRAINS	A.M.	A.M.	A.M.	P.M.	P.M.	P.M.	
Lv. Salem...............	3.10	10.13	11.43	6.55	11.25	*11.54	....
Ar. Eugene.............	6.00	11.59	1.50	9.10	1.20	1.40	
Ar. Roseburg...........	....	2.35	....	....	4.25		
Ar. Ashland............		8.05	....		11.05		

FROM THE SOUTH

MOTOR COACHES	A.M.	A.M.	A.M.	A.M.	P.M.	A.M.	P.M.
Lv. Ashland............		....	....	....		6.30	....
Lv. Roseburg...........		....	6.45	....		11.32	....
Lv. Eugene.............		7.30	9.40	10.30	....	2.31	4.30
Lv. Corvallis..........	7.00	9.00	....	11.55	3.00	3.55	5.57
Ar. Salem..............	8.25	10.30	12.10	1.32	4.28	5.25	7.43
TRAINS	P.M.	A.M.	P.M.	P.M.	P.M.	A.M.	
Lv. Ashland............	6.05	....	....	....		11.05	....
Lv. Roseburg..........	12.01	....	....	....		4.15	
Lv. Eugene.............	3.25	4.50	*12.50	3.00	4.20	6.40	....
Ar. Salem..............	5.25	6.40	2.29	4.55	6.05	8.19	....

*Extra Fare Train.

Another Convenience. Southern Pacific rail tickets may be used on the Silver Gray Motor Coaches—go one way and return the other if you wish.

Order and send your small packages on the **"Silver Gray"**
DEPENDABLE SERVICE, LOW RATES

This is one of Southern Pacific's famous "cab in front" locomotives. Some people call the 4-8-8-2 locomotives "back up" locomotives, but their real name is "Articulated-Consolidation." They were built so engineers and firemen could see farther down the track which made for greater safety around curves and through tunnels and snowsheds in the mountains. This locomotive is really two engines combined into one. This photo was taken in the 1940s.

The big and the little: *Right*, SP No. 3631 (2-10-2), a heavy freight locomotive weighing 549,600 pounds. The smaller train is SP No. 1 (4-2-4), an early wood burner weighing 39,000 pounds.

THE NORTHERN PACIFIC RAILROAD

IN SEPTEMBER OF 1883 the Northern Pacific Railroad (NP) was completed and was the first transcontinental line into the Pacific Northwest area, opening up many of the northern states from St. Paul to the Columbia River and Puget Sound. It ended Portland's isolation from the east.

The last spike celebration for the Northern Pacific Railroad was held at Gold Creek, Montana on September 8, 1883. This photo shows one of the four trains that brought visiting dignitaries to Portland, including ex-President U.S. Grant, to help celebrate the completion of the line. The locomotive is a 4-4-0 American Standard wood burner. The only identifiable person in the photo is James Thomas Walsh, who later became superintendent of the Oregon Pacific Railway. He can be seen near the tender of the locomotive with his hands behind him and without a tie.

In its 1883 issue, the *West Shore*, an Oregon magazine printed in Portland, covered the arrival of the Northern Pacific Railway into Portland.

Building the Northern Pacific Railway: The engineering party at the east end of the Wallace, Idaho yard on October 15, 1889. Standing *left to right:* Fred Love, Harvey Dunn, William H. Adamson and Bert C. Wilson. Seated *left to right:* First man unknown, Fred Schneible, Carlos Call, Fred Gillman, and the rest are unknown.

NP No. 1, the "Minnetonka," built by Smith and Porter of Pittsburgh in 1870 costing $6,700. It was used in construction work on the main line in Minnesota during the 1870s. It was then shipped to the West Coast for construction work in building the line from Kalama to Tacoma in Washington. It is twenty-eight and one-half feet long, weighs eighteen tons and is still in excellent operating condition for exhibits.

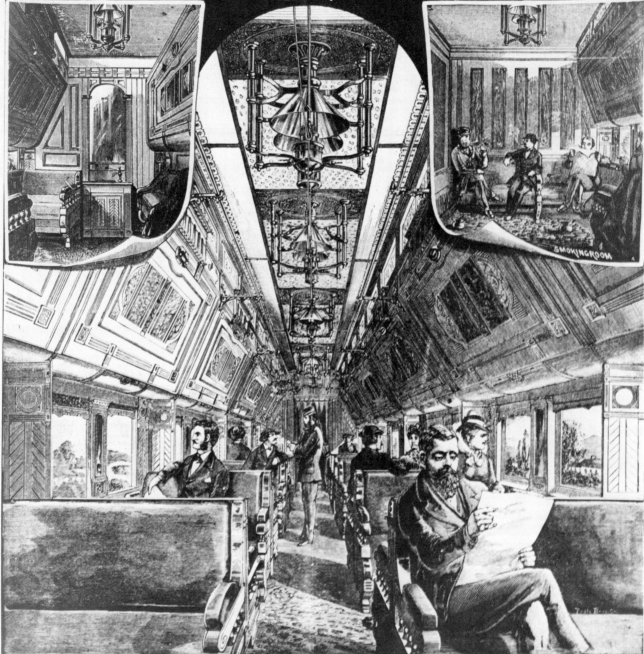

An 1884 advertisement for the "Atlantic Express," a Pullman sleeper car which ran through from Portland to St. Paul. The Oregon Railway & Navigation Company handled trains from Portland to Wallula Junction and the NP handled trains from Wallula Junction to St. Paul.

APRIL 1884 SCHEDULE:

Lv. Portland	OR&N No. 2 Atlantic Express	7:30 A.M.	Monday
Ar. Wallula Junction	OR&N No. 2 Atlantic Express	7:30 P.M.	Monday
Lv. Wallula Junction	NP No. 2 Atlantic Express	8:00 P.M.	Monday
Ar. St. Paul	NP No. 2 Atlantic Express	12:25 P.M.	Friday

Dining Cars.

The Northern Pacific Railroad is now equipped with a line of the finest Dining Cars on the Continent, in which first-class meals are served at

75 Cents Each.

These Cars are new, from the Pullman Car Works, built expressly for this Company, and will be run and operated exclusively by the Northern Pacific Railroad Company, under the direction of an efficient and experienced Superintendent.

Tourists, prospectors, and all classes of the traveling public, will at once recognize this as one of the leading features of this already popular route to Minnesota, Dakota and Montana; and will appreciate the comforts to be derived from this specially attractive feature in modern travel.

To eat when you feel like it, and get what you want,
Is the traveler's enjoyment when taking a jaunt;
Therefore, Tourists, Sportsmen and others, who are on the look out
For solid comfort in traveling, and a picturesque route,
Take the NORTHERN PACIFIC and in Dining Cars fine,
Enjoy the YELLOWSTONE ROUTE and MONTANA SHORT LINE.

HORTON RECLINING CHAIR CARS BETWEEN FARGO AND MANDAN.

An advertisement for the new dining cars featured by the Northern Pacific Railroad

Migration Into the West

The heaviest movement of colonist trains started near the turn of the century. The railroads lowered the one-way rate from the East to the West in order to encourage immigration and create new traffic. During the next few years both foreign-born and our own Americans living in the East came west to locate and settle.

The first colonist trains used were old-fashioned, dilapidated day coaches that had been transformed into lounging, eating, sleeping and living quarters for the colonists' use while traveling. One could hear snoring at almost any hour of the day while the night was broken into all of the varied noises that train jerking, uncomfortable beds and bad air can create.

Most of the people using this service were middle or lower class residents of that day along with the many foreign arrivals that had passed through Ellis Island Immigration Station. The inconvenience of these cars was accepted, considering the saving of rail fare involved which would help towards establishing residence in the West.

The solicitation folders and various types of advertising material printed by the railroads and the Chambers of Commerce, were distributed by the thousands with the appealing message of "Go West Young Man" and build a home on cheap or free lands. The NP was probably the first railroad company in Oregon to encourage westward migration through the use of such advertising.

A typical colonist sleeper train used by the many emigrants at the turn of the century

The Demonstration Train was used for the entire Pacific Northwest. Each railroad would use its own locomotive and crew, but the train remained intact. The people are boarding at Springfield, Oregon on a Southern Pacific line.

Demonstration Trains

Demonstration Trains were an outgrowth of the colonists' traffic. The railroads began to realize that the success of the colonizing movement was measured not by the number of people that came west but by the number that "stuck" and the degree of their success. They felt traffic would come to their lines along with increased valuation returns to the community, not when they located a man and his family but when they made them into successful producers.

There was much in the way of resources and methods in the West that was entirely new to the average colonists. Irrigation was a new science having different applications in each community. Highly specialized fruit growing was another new field. The railroads and commercial bodies began helping these people to understand these various problems.

One of the favorite methods used to edu-cate the emigrants was the Demonstration Trains. The railroads furnished the train equipment, the state agriculture college sent along experts and the commercial bodies helped with the advertising. There were about thirty employees on each train. One car was devoted to horticulture, still another to setting up a model dairy barn and poultry house. Many were interested in the resources of timber, minerals, water power and the like, all things that would make them better settlers for this land. The experts would lecture on different subjects according to the needs of the community.

The train made about four station stops in a day along with a mass meeting held at night.

Someone once said, "The West was re-making the colonists and most certainly the colonists were remaking the West."

NP Reaches Portland

In 1883 the Northern Pacific Railroad reached Portland by using the Oregon Railway and Navigation (OR&N) tracks from Wallula Junction to Portland, a line that followed the south side of the Columbia River. At Portland the NP had previously built its own right-of-way to Tacoma and Seattle via Goble, Oregon and Kalama, Washington.

In 1887 the NP again reached Tacoma and Seattle, this time by continuing its track-laying program entirely in Washington Territory passing through such cities as Yakima and Ellensburg. The OR&N was soon to become property of the Union Pacific (UP), a line that would be competitive with the NP.

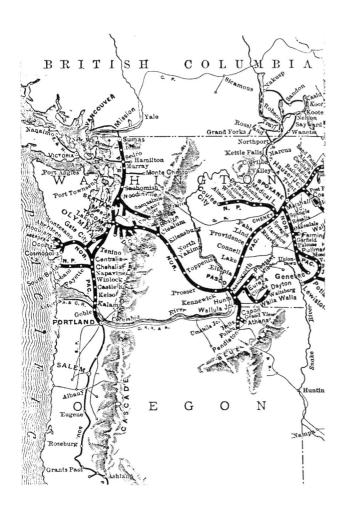

Goble, Oregon was a busy switching area in 1888. NP locomotive No. 329 is on hand to assist in switching trains onto *The Tacoma*.

The Tacoma carried trains, including their locomotives, across the Columbia River, from Goble, Oregon to Kalama, Washington in 1888.

1891 Schedule:

Lv. Portland	NP No. 2 Atlantic Mail	7:00 A.M.	Monday
Ar. Goble	NP No. 2 Atlantic Mail	8:30 A.M.	Monday
Lv. Goble by ferry	*The Tacoma*	8:35 A.M.	Monday
Ar. Kalama, Wash.	*The Tacoma*	9:00 A.M.	Monday
Lv. Kalama	NP No. 2 Atlantic Mail	9:10 A.M.	Monday
Ar. St. Paul	NP No. 2 Atlantic Mail	6:05 P.M.	Friday
Ar. Chicago	NP No. 2 Atlantic Mail	9:30 A.M.	Saturday

The "Atlantic Mail" in 1891

The year 1891 was the first year the Northern Pacific trains from Portland to St. Paul and Chicago were routed through Tacoma rather than by way of the OR&N route along the Columbia River. This was also the first year a Pullman car was used from Portland to Chicago. Beyond St. Paul travelers used the Wisconsin Central and the Milwaukee Railroads.

Northern Pacific Advertisements

1891–92–93 SCHEDULE:

Lv. Portland	NP No. 4 Atlantic Express	10:00 P. M.	Monday
Lv. Tacoma	NP No. 4 Atlantic Express	7:10 A. M.	Tuesday
Ar. St. Paul	NP No. 4 Atlantic Express	12:40 P. M.	Friday
Lv. St. Paul	Milwaukee No. 2, Atlantic Express	1:40 P. M.	Friday
Ar. Chicago	Milwaukee No. 2, Atlantic Express	7:00 A. M.	Saturday

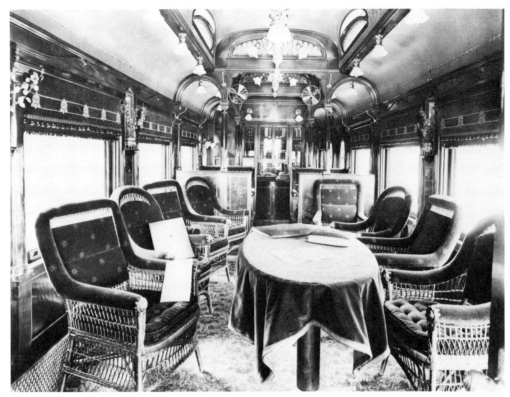

A Northern Pacific observation car

A Northern Pacific dining car

A Northern Pacific sleeping car

An advertisement for the "North Coast Limited" in 1904

The "North Coast Limited" at Livingston, Montana

1904 SCHEDULE:

Lv. Portland	NP No. 2 North Coast Limited	2:00 P.M.	Monday
Lv. Tacoma	NP No. 2 North Coast Limited	7:35 P.M.	Monday
Ar. St. Paul	NP No. 2 North Coast Limited	2:30 P.M.	Thursday

The "Northern Pacific Express" carries a sleeper to Yellowstone National Park in 1910. The NP park train is pulling into Gardiner, Montana — the gateway to Yellowstone National Park. It is pulled by engine No. 336 and has been carried through from St. Paul. This train was later called the "Comet."

1910 Schedule:

Lv. Chicago	Burlington RR	9:20 A.M.	Sunday
Ar. St. Paul	Burlington RR	9:15 P.M.	Sunday
Lv. St. Paul	NP No. 3 Northern Pacific Express	10:15 P.M.	Sunday
Ar. Livingston, Mont.	NP No. 3 Northern Pacific Express	4:30 A.M.	Tuesday
Lv. Livingston	NP No. 103 Passenger	4:35 A.M.	Tuesday
Ar. Gardiner, Mont.	NP No. 103 Passenger	10:00 A.M.	Tuesday

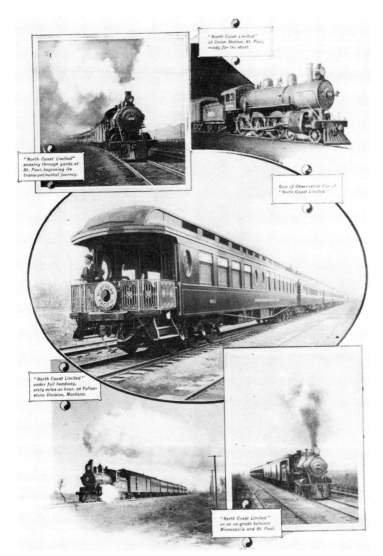

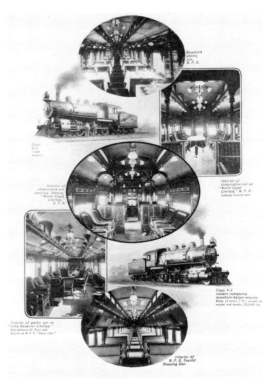

The "North Coast Limited" in 1910. This sleeper train carried passengers through from Portland to St. Paul and from Seattle to Chicago. Car-to-car change at Spokane was necessary for those en route from Portland to Chicago. The North Bank line was opened for service from Portland to Pasco, Washington on March 11, 1908 and to Spokane on May 3, 1909. This line was built along the north side of the Columbia River and was used by the Spokane Portland & Seattle Railway (SPS), a subsidiary of the GN and NP.

1910 SCHEDULE:

Lv. Portland	SPS No. 2 North Coast Limited	8:45 A.M.	Sunday
Ar. Spokane, Wash.	SPS No. 2 North Coast Limited	9:25 P.M.	Sunday
Lv. Spokane	NP No. 2 North Coast Limited	9:55 P.M.	Sunday
Ar. St. Paul	NP No. 2 North Coast Limited	10:00 P.M.	Tuesday
Ar. Chicago	CB&Q No. 2 North Coast Limited	11:00 A.M.	Wednesday

NP No. 434, the "Fast Mail," passing through Kelso, Washington. Note that the orderboard is "down" on the left side signaling the train to pass through without stopping.

1915 SCHEDULE:

Lv. Portland	NP No. 434 Fast Mail	4:10 P.M.	Monday
Ar. Kelso, Wash.	NP No. 434 Fast Mail	6:01 P.M.	Monday
Ar. Seattle	NP No. 434 Fast Mail	10:45 P.M.	Monday

NP No. 25, the "Passenger," stopping at Oakville, Washington for passengers and to unload mail and express. It is pulled by locomotive No. 235 (4-6-0). Notice the one-ton Reo truck backed against the railroad station unloading milk cans for movement on the train.

1920 SCHEDULE:

Lv. Portland	NP No. 8 Passenger	8:30 A.M.	Monday
Ar. Centralia, Wash.	NP No. 8 Passenger	12:35 P.M.	Monday
Lv. Centralia	NP No. 25 Passenger	1:00 P.M.	Monday
Ar. Oakville, Wash.	NP No. 25 Passenger	1:57 P.M.	Monday

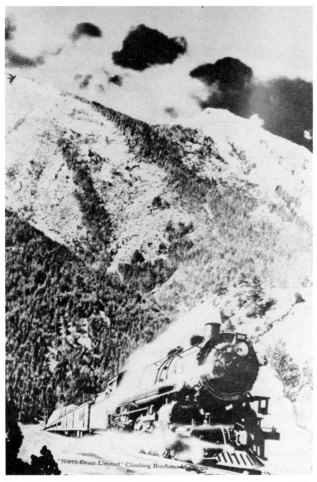

The "North Coast Limited" climbing Bozeman Mountain in
about 1925.

"North Coast" advertising

NP No. 2, the "North Coast Limited," in Portland in 1935 showing the new equipment to be used. This was the first locomotive
to use roller bearings. This through train carried passengers from Portland to Chicago in 1935.

Ten Cents
now buys a
Great Big
Baked Potato
on the

NEW NORTH COAST LIMITED
CHICAGO • SAINT PAUL • MINNEAPOLIS • NORTH PACIFIC COAST

Prices of other foods also have been materially reduced on North Coast Limited diners, but Northern Pacific quality and service are maintained.

E. E. Nelson
Passenger Traffic Manager
Northern Pacific Railway

The picture on the inside fold shows the actual size of the average Big Baked Potato

Left, a Northern Pacific Advertisement

Right, little girl, BIG baked potato! An NP trademark

Northern Pacific Advertising

"Main Line Freight" taking on water at Sumner, Washington in 1938 pulled by locomotive No. 1812 (2-8-2)

NP engine No. 4018 being refueled under a coal chute at Puyallup, Washington in 1939 during the last days of steam operation. These engines were called "twenty-wheelers" and were capable of pulling as many loaded freight cars as the draft-gear of the cars would stand. They were ninety-four feet long and were a combination of two complete locomotives. Note the coal chute: engines could reload on either side of the chute up the steep incline into the bin. Two or three section men were responsible for keeping the bins ready for use at all times and to see that large chunks of coal were broken into small pieces before being dumped into the locomotive tender. Any piece larger than six inches could not be used in the firebox of an engine. There was a constant "war" between men who manned the coal chutes and engine men over the size of the coal pieces furnished.

Left, the "Vista-Dome North Coast Limited" in 1952 which featured new deluxe-chair cars. The gray-haired man next to the window is Harry Wilson Shields.

Right, "Vista-Dome" train travel

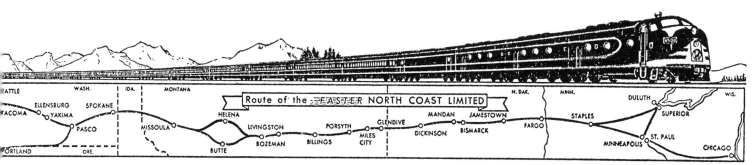

Route of the FASTER NORTH COAST LIMITED

You'll Like the *Faster* NORTH COAST LIMITED

NORTHERN PACIFIC'S famous transcontinental streamliner, The North Coast Limited, goes on a new fast schedule beginning Sunday, November 16.

The Chicago-Seattle run will be made in 46½ hours in both directions, a reduction of 12 hours westbound and 9¼ hours eastbound. The new Chicago-Portland westbound time is 46 hours, which is 12 hours less, and eastbound 44¾ hours, a cut of 11¾ hours.

Between St. Paul and Seattle the new time is 39½ hours and between Minneapolis and Seattle 39 hours. The St. Paul-Portland time is 39 hours westbound and 37¾ hours eastbound, and the Minneapolis-Portland time is half an hour less.

Convenient Connections are provided by the new schedule—at Chicago with the principal name trains east and south, and at Portland with Southern Pacific streamliners to and from California.

DOME CARS COMING—We are ordering 16 magnificent Vista-Dome cars for the North Coast Limited—three Domes for each train. When these luxurious cars are received, travelers will be able to enjoy the full grandeur of Northern Pacific's famed scenic route.

THE NEW *FASTER* SCHEDULE OF THE NORTH COAST LIMITED

EASTBOUND—Train 26   Effective Nov. 16, 1952   WESTBOUND—Train 25

EASTBOUND—Train 26			WESTBOUND—Train 25		
Lv. Seattle	1:15 pm	Sun.	Lv. Chicago (CB&Q)	11:30 am	Sun.
Lv. Tacoma	12:55 pm	"	Lv. St. Paul (NP)	6:30 pm	"
Lv. Portland	3:00 pm	"	Lv. Minneapolis	7:00 pm	"
Lv. Ellensburg	4:45 pm	"	Lv. Duluth	5:05 pm	"
Lv. Yakima	5:50 pm	"	Lv. Superior	5:17 pm	"
Lv. Pasco	7:45 pm	"	Lv. Staples	9:21 pm	"
Lv. Spokane	10:30 pm	"	Lv. Fargo	11:25 pm	"
Lv. Missoula (MST)	5:00 am	Mon.	Lv. Jamestown	1:06 am	Mon.
Lv. Helena	7:10 am	Mon.	Lv. Bismarck	2:49 am	"
Lv. Butte	7:17 am	Mon.	Lv. Mandan (MST)	2:11 am	"
Lv. Bozeman	9:56 am	"	Lv. Dickinson	4:00 am	"
Lv. Livingston	10:51 am	"	Ar. Glendive	5:57 am	"
Lv. Billings	12:58 pm	"	Ar. Miles City	7:29 am	"
Lv. Forsyth	2:49 pm	"	Ar. Forsyth	8:27 am	"
Lv. Miles City	3:42 pm	"	Ar. Billings	10:23 am	"
Lv. Glendive	5:15 pm	"	Ar. Livingston	12:30 pm	"
Lv. Dickinson	7:15 pm	"	Ar. Bozeman	1:30 pm	"
Lv. Mandan (CST)	10:07 pm	"	Ar. Helena	4:05 pm	Mon.
Lv. Bismarck	10:19 pm	"	Ar. Butte	4:04 pm	Mon.
Lv. Jamestown	12:07 am	Tue.	Ar. Missoula	6:20 pm	"
Lv. Fargo	1:47 am	"	Ar. Spokane (PST)	10:45 pm	"
Ar. Staples	3:44 am	"	Ar. Pasco	1:30 am	Tue.
Ar. Superior	7:39 am	Tue.	Ar. Yakima	3:20 am	"
Ar. Duluth	7:55 am	"	Ar. Ellensburg	4:21 am	"
Ar. Minneapolis	6:10 am	Tue.	Ar. Portland	7:30 am	"
Ar. St. Paul	6:40 am	"	Ar. Tacoma	8:00 am	"
Ar. Chicago (CB&Q)	1:45 pm		Ar. Seattle	8:00 am	"

ACCOMMODATIONS—The faster North Coast Limited equipment will be modern, light-weight, matched cars—all-room Pullmans with duplex roomettes, roomettes, bedrooms and compartments, luxurious Pullman-Observation car, "Day-Nite" and day coaches, coach-buffet-lounge car and dining car. *All coach seats will be reserved.*

THE CASCADE DIVISION

OF THE

Northern Pacific Railroad

WILL BE COMPLETED IN THE MONTH OF

1887----JUNE----1887.

EMIGRANTS, NOTE THIS!

For the better accommodation of Emigrant Passengers, they are carried nearly the entire distance between St. Paul, Minn., and Helena, Mon., on daily Express Trains, thus

REDUCING THE EMIGRANT TIME Between St. Paul and Portland,

TO ABOUT

6 DAYS,

WITHOUT CHANGE OF CARS.

BEAR IN MIND that the Northern Pacific is the only railroad running Emigrant Sleepers from the East into Montana, Oregon and Washington Territory.

From the NP public timetable, Spring 1884

The completion of this road gives to Tacoma, the western terminus of the Northern Pacific Railroad, direct communication with Eastern Washington and the East.

The citizens of Tacoma will celebrate the event on July 4th, 1887, with appropriate festivities and ceremonies.

Special rates have been given by the Northern Pacific Railroad Company to those who wish to attend the celebration, and the citizens of Tacoma extend an invitation to all to come and enjoy themselves, and at the same time see the most rapidly-growing city in the Northwest.

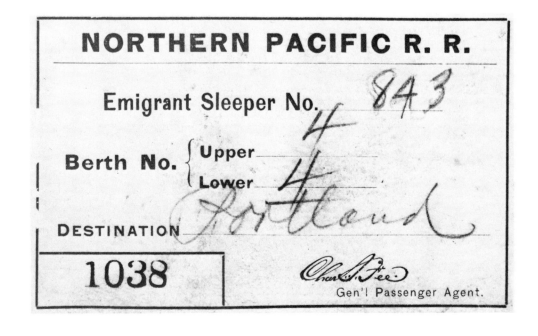

NORTHERN PACIFIC R. R.

Emigrant Sleeper No. 843

Berth No. { Upper 4
            { Lower 4

DESTINATION Portland

1038

Gen'l Passenger Agent.

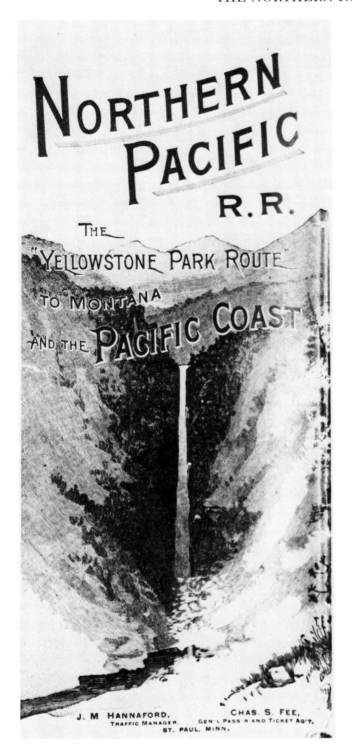

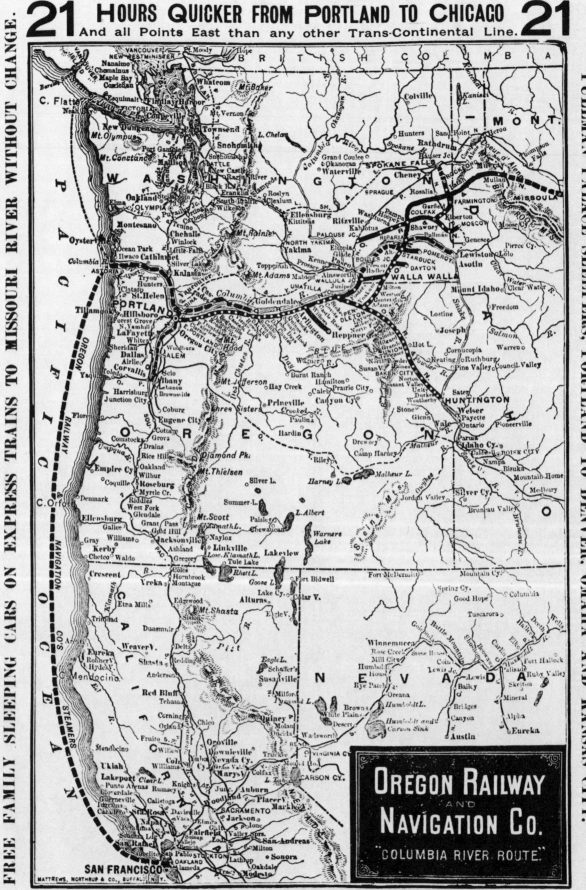

21 HOURS QUICKER FROM PORTLAND TO CHICAGO **21**
And all Points East than any other Trans-Continental Line.

FREE FAMILY SLEEPING CARS ON EXPRESS TRAINS TO MISSOURI RIVER WITHOUT CHANGE.

PULLMAN PALACE SLEEPERS, PORTLAND TO DENVER, OMAHA AND KANSAS CITY.

OREGON RAILWAY
AND
NAVIGATION CO.
"COLUMBIA RIVER ROUTE."

THE OREGON RAILWAY & NAVIGATION COMPANY
and
THE UNION PACIFIC RAILROAD COMPANY

THE BEGINNING of what is today the Union Pacific Railroad in Oregon is traceable from an original document carefully preserved in the records in Omaha bearing the date of August 29, 1857. This unique paper is a lease for the right-of-way for a railroad from the landing known as the Wasco Steamboat Landing claim, now the village of Cascade Locks.

A wagon road was constructed between

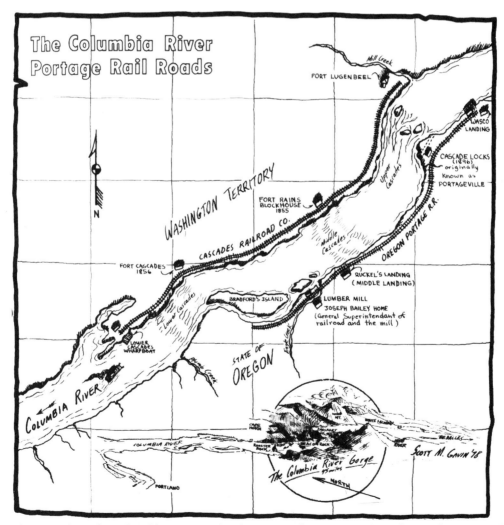

This map shows how the old portage railroads were used in conjunction with steamboats up and down the Columbia River where land passages were more easily negotiated than water.

A scene along the lower portion of the four and one-half-mile portage railroad extending below Joseph Bailey's Mill to Wasco Landing. The rails are squared timber planks about five feet apart and were in use two years before the "Oregon Pony" came on the scene. The man in the white shirt is Joseph Bailey.

the "middle landing" or "middle cascades" near Joseph H. Ruckells' residence on the riverbank above Eagle Creek, about one mile east of the present Bonneville.

Most of the traffic between Portland and The Dalles went over the older portage on the north bank of the river at the rapids where a land passage was more easily negotiated. But the owners on the Oregon side were resolved to surpass the facilities of their rivals by providing a railway four and one-half miles long which would extend a short distance below Joseph Bailey's Mill to the Wasco Landing terminus of the portage on the south side of the Columbia River. They obtained their objective before midsummer of 1859, though the railway was built very cheaply. In places it suffered severely each year of its life during the high water stages of the river. Much of it was constructed on timber trestlework. Four or five diminutive, horse drawn cars constituted the equipment used in construction. The rails were squared timbers placed about five feet apart.

In 1861 the proprietors of the portage on the Oregon side took another step forward. A locomotive was ordered from the Vulcan Iron Works in San Francisco. "The Oregon Pony" was the first steam locomotive built on the Pacific Coast and is reported to have been the first in use in the Pacific Northwest.

"The Pony" arrived in Portland by ship from San Francisco in 1862 and began operating in May of the same year. As one party detailed the movement of "The Pony," "The portage of the cascades, heretofore so great a bugbear in the trip from The Dalles to Portland, is now made in a brief hour on the cars, without detriment or danger. An extra dollar for riding on the cars is charged, though if you prefer you can walk on the road in nearly the same time, free of cost."

Another portage was built on the Oregon side and opened April 20, 1863 from The Dalles to Celilo, a thirteen-mile distance which had been established as the transfer point to and from the upper river steamboats. Its construction in 1862–63 has made The Dalles-Celilo line the oldest portion of the Union Pacific Railroad. The previously mentioned portage at Bonneville would have been the oldest but it ceased to function in 1863 and it would be another twenty years before Henry Villard would construct the Oregon Railway & Navigation Company at the same location.

The Oregon Pony

Built in San Francisco by the Vulcan Iron Foundry in 1858–59, "The Oregon Pony" was the first locomotive built on the Pacific Coast and the first used north of the California state line. It was brought to Portland by the S.S. *Pacific* on March 31, 1862 and operated around the rapids of the Columbia River between Bonneville and Cascade Locks. On its first trip, May 10, 1862, a band of some three hundred Indians filled with curiosity watched while their chief was offered a ride. He was a steady passenger thereafter for nearly one year. "The Pony" weighed 9700 pounds and had a speed of about ten miles per hour.

"The Oregon Pony" was the first locomotive built on the Pacific Coast. It was built in San Francisco in the late 1850s

Here is a scene of the oldest portion of track on the entire Union Pacific system. It is the thirteen-mile portage railroad built between The Dalles and Celilo. On April 20, 1863, the Oregon Steam Navigation Company began to operate this five-foot gauge railroad served by the connecting steamboat lines on the Columbia River above and below the unnavigable section of the river.

This little engine was built by Danforth & Cooke Locomotive Foundry and was brought around the Horn in 1863 to reach Oregon.

Steamer *Oneonta* at the Lower Cascades on the Washington side of the Columbia River in 1867, ready to depart for Portland as soon as passengers are transferred from the westbound Cascade Portage Railroad (seen approaching). The Cascade Portage Railroad is bringing passengers and freight from the Upper Cascades, which arrived to that point by steamer from The Dalles. The steamer *Oneonta* was built at the Cascades and follows a Mississippi River style made famous by Mark Twain in his many riverboat stories. The steamer is 182 feet long.

OREGON STEAM NAVIGATION COMPANY.

The Oregon Steam Navigation Company's

Steamer "Oneonta,"
CAPTAIN JOHN WOLF,

Will leave Portland daily, (Sundays excepted) at 5 A. M., connecting with the

CASCADE RAILROAD,

And **Steamer "Idaho,"** Capt. JOHN McNULTY, arriving at THE DALLES at 4 P. M., same day.

Steamers "Yakima," "Tenino" and "Owyhee,"
CAPTAINS T. J. STUMP AND S. D. HOLMES,

Will leave CELILO on TUESDAY, THURSDAY and SATURDAY, (on arrival of the morning train from the Dalles) for UMATILLA and WALLULA, proceeding as far as LEWISTON during high water in the Snake River.

FOR ASTORIA.
Steamers "Dixie Thompson" and "Okanagon,"
CAPTAIN H. A. SNOW,

Will leave PORTLAND at 6 A. M., on MONDAY, WEDNESDAY and FRIDAY, arriving at ASTORIA same day at 6 P. M.

FOR MONTICELLO.
Steamers "Fannie Troup" and "Rescue,"
CAPTAINS W. H. SMITH AND RICHARD HOYT,

Leave PORTLAND daily (except Sunday) at 6 A. M., arriving at MONTICELLO at 11:30 A. M., connecting with daily stages for OLYMPIA, Washington Territory.

January, 1871.   **J. C. AINSWORTH,**
THEODORE WYGANT, Sec'y.   **President.**

1866 SCHEDULE:

Lv. Portland	Steamer *Oneonta*	5:00 A.M.	Monday
Ar. Lower Cascades	Steamer *Oneonta*	11:00 A.M.	Monday
Lv. Lower Cascades	Cascade Portage Railroad	11:05 A.M.	Monday
Ar. Upper Cascades	Cascade Portage Railroad	12:00 P.M.	Monday
Lv. Upper Cascades	Steamer *Idaho*	12:05 P.M.	Monday
Ar. The Dalles	Steamer *Idaho*	4:00 P.M.	Monday

Sleeper Service in Oregon

The first Pullman sleeping car service on any line west of Ogden, Utah started June 21, 1881, running between The Dalles and Walla Walla, Washington. The Central Pacific Railway in California operated much lighter cars known as Silver Palace sleeping cars. Incidents herewith were related by William H. Boot, one of the first Pullman conductors, who until his passing, resided in Salem.

Early in 1880 when Henry Villard was building the Oregon Railway & Navigation Company up the Columbia River he invited George Mortimer Pullman, the sleeping car magnate who had become financially interested in the OR&N's projected system of railways in Oregon and eastern Washington, to visit the great Oregon country and see for himself the progress and growth of this area.

When George Pullman returned East he immediately ordered his own Pullman Company to start construction on four ten-section one drawing room sleeping cars. He named them "The Oregon," "The Umatilla," "The Walla Walla" and "The Wallula."

Getting these sleeping cars to The Dalles was not an easy task in the 1880s. The cars were brought west over the Union Pacific-Central Pacific tracks into San Francisco. With much difficulty, two of these large and heavy sleeping cars were placed on the deck of the bark *Tam O'Shanter* at San Francisco and by water arrived in Portland during the middle of June 1881. From here they moved by steamboat down the Willamette River to the portage line tracks at the Cascades. After a six-mile trip over a standard gauge portage line to the Upper Cascades, these two sleepers, "The Oregon" and "The Wallula," were loaded on the barge *The Atlas* and towed into The Dalles.

The night of June 21, 1881 was the beginning of Pullman service in the Pacific Northwest. It was on this night that the sleeper "The Oregon" first traveled from Walla Walla to The Dalles, meeting the sleeper "The Wallula" which had originated in The Dalles and was bound for Walla Walla.

Before the service had begun the editor of *The Dalles Times* inspected the two new Pullman cars and reported in his newspaper of that date, "We were shown through the Pullman Palace cars yesterday by the Pullman Conductor and they are indeed a valuable addition to the rolling stock of the road. The berths are arranged on both sides of the car, one being fastened in a shelf above the head during the day and the other forming a comfortable bed for the night. The work is in the highest style of the art and fine inlaid carving. It is the prettiest we have seen. Attached to these are all of the necessary closets and toilet rooms for ladies and gentlemen while mirrors surround one on every hand."

A Pullman sleeper car of the 1880s, similar to that of "The Wallula" and "The Oregon"

The Atlantic Express

The "Atlantic Express," which carried the first Pullman sleeper car down the OR&N tracks in 1881, consisted of U.S. Mail, a baggage car, coaches and the sleeper "Wallula." Below is the schedule of the first Pullman trip.

1881 SCHEDULE:

Lv. The Dalles	OR&N No. 2 Atlantic Express	8:00 P.M.	Monday
Ar. Walla Walla	OR&N No. 2 Atlantic Express	7:00 A.M.	Tuesday

Pullman sleepers ran from Portland to Pendleton on September 11, 1882 and from Portland to Walla Walla on November 20, 1882. The train consisted of a baggage and mail car, three coaches and Pullman car "The Oregon." The train's conductor was Edward Lyons and the engineer was Andrew Curtis.

1882 SCHEDULE:

Lv. Portland	OR&N No. 2 Atlantic Express	5:00 P.M.	Monday
Ar. Walla Walla	OR&N No. 2 Atlantic Express	4:00 P.M.	Tuesday

The Pullman sleepers also ran from Portland to La Grande on June 16, 1884 and into Baker on August 18, 1884. They ran into Huntington on November 10, 1884 where they connected with the Oregon Short Line on November 25, 1884. Trains later ran through from Portland to Omaha on December 1, 1884.

The Pullman sleepers were carried through from Portland to Council Bluffs, Iowa on April 1, 1886.

1886 SCHEDULE:

Lv. Portland	OR&N No. 2 Atlantic Express	3:30 P.M.	Sunday
Ar. Umatilla Junction	OR&N No. 2 Atlantic Express	1:25 A.M.	Monday
Lv. Umatilla Junction	OR&N No. 6 Atlantic Express	2:00 A.M.	Monday
Ar. Council Bluffs, Iowa	OR&N No. 6 Atlantic Express	8:15 A.M.	Thursday

Drawing room of a Pullman car

Interior of a Pullman sleeping car

The "Fast Mail" in 1891 westbound in the Columbia River Gorge area pulled by engine No. 80 (4-4-0)

1891 SCHEDULE:

Lv. Council Bluffs, Iowa	UP No. 1 Fast Mail	7:00 P.M.	Sunday
Ar. Mulnomah Falls, Oreg.	UP No. 1 Fast Mail	7:28 A.M.	Wednesday
Ar. Portland	UP No. 1 Fast Mail	9:00 A.M.	Wednesday

OR&N No. 4, "The Spokane Flyer," which ran daily in 1900, is pulled by OR&N No. 73 (4-4-0) and is stopping at Bridal Veil, Oregon to take on water.

1900 SCHEDULE:

Lv. Portland	OR&N No. 4 Spokane Flyer	6:00 P.M.	Sunday
Ar. Bridal Veil, Oreg.	OR&N No. 4 Spokane Flyer	6:56 P.M.	Sunday
Ar. Spokane, Wash.	OR&N No. 4 Spokane Flyer	9:00 A.M.	Monday

A brakeman stands waiting shortly before the departure of "The Spokane Flyer." Notice the open vestibule cars.

OR&N No. 2, "The Chicago-Portland Special," is pulled by engine No. 81 (4-4-0). This photo was taken near The Dalles.

1901 SCHEDULE:

Lv. Portland	OR&N No. 2 Chicago-Portland Special	9:00 A.M.	Sunday
Ar. The Dalles	OR&N No. 2 Chicago-Portland Special	12:30 P.M.	Sunday
Ar. Chicago	OR&N No. 2 Chicago-Portland Special	9:30 A.M.	Thursday

This photo was taken somewhere along the Sumpter Valley Railroad. The train is pulled by Sumpter Valley's locomotive No. 6 (2-6-0). The Sumpter Valley Railroad connected with the Union Pacific at Baker City in 1905.

UP No. 8, "The Spokane Passenger," near Walla Walla, Washington in about 1909 pulled by coal burning engine No. 609 (4-4-0). The train has taken the siding for a meet with one coming in the opposite direction. The spool-like contraption in back of the bell is a generator supplying electricity for the converted electric headlight. The engine was originally equipped with a carbonate lamp and in changing over from gas burning carbonate to electricity, the same shell casing for the headlight has been retained. The railroad book of rules required that any night train meeting another coming in the opposite direction cannot be passed if its headlights cannot be seen. Trains entering the siding, as soon as they are in the clear, must turn off their headlight. Note the rolled up screen above the headlight. In order to avoid relighting the carbonate lamp, which in the past had caused some injuries, the firemen would just pull down the blind, which worked like a window shade on a spring, to cover the headlight. The blind has never been removed but dimming the electric light was later performed inside the cab of the locomotive. Notice, too, the coal-dock behind the last car.

1909 SCHEDULE:

Lv. Pendleton, Oreg.	UP No. 8 Spokane Passenger	12:30 P.M.	Monday
Ar. Walla Walla, Wash.	UP No. 8 Spokane Passenger	2:15 P.M.	Monday
Ar. Spokane, Wash.	UP No. 8 Spokane Passenger	11:00 P.M.	Monday

"The Oregon-Washington Limited," a train name used regularly from 1909 to 1921, is pulled by engine No. 3212 (4-6-2), Pacific-type. This photo was taken along the Columbia River highway. Note the forked rail directly in front of the locomotive. This is a safety device placed on all bridges and trestles in the event that one of the trucks (wheels) jumps the rail, the second track will prevent the engine from turning over.

1914 Schedule:

Lv. Portland	UP No. 18 Oregon-Washington Limited	10:00 A.M.	Sunday
Ar. Chicago	UP No. 18 Oregon-Washington Limited	11:00 A.M.	Wednesday

Oregon-Washington Railroad a Navigation Co. (OWR&N) No. 2, the "Pendleton Local," stopped at Biggs, Hermiston and Stanfield in 1913. In this photo the "Pendleton Local" is pulled by engine No. 94 (4-4-2). The train in the center is Columbia Southern (CS) No. 1 making a connection at Biggs.

1913 Schedule:

Lv. Portland	OWR&N No. 2 Pendleton Local	7:50 A.M.	Sunday
Ar. Biggs	OWR&N No. 2 Pendleton Local	12:05 P.M.	Sunday
Ar. Hermiston	OWR&N No. 2 Pendleton Local	3:10 P.M.	Sunday
Ar. Stanfield	OWR&N No. 2 Pendleton Local	3:30 P.M.	Sunday
Ar. Pendleton	OWR&N No. 2 Pendleton Local	4:35 P.M.	Sunday

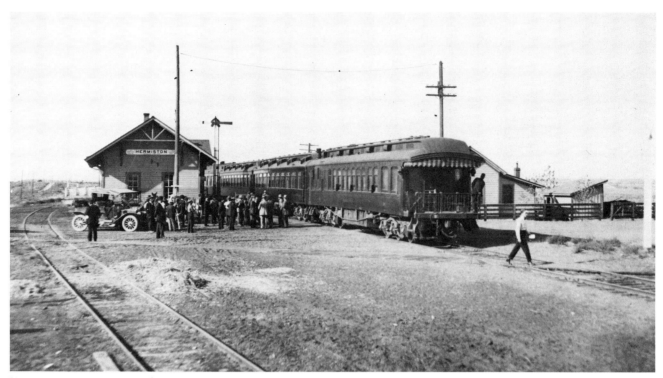

Hermiston Station in 1913. The station order board is "red," signaling the train to stop for passengers or train orders. A 1912 White automobile can be seen in front of the railroad station.

This photo was taken in front of a grain elevator in Stanfield, probably a cleaning plant. Three pair of horses with two mules in the lead position pull a heavy load of sacked grains. "Tump line" is fastened to the bit of the lead mule which acts as a signal cord. One pull of the line and the mule will direct the wagon to the right, two pulls he will go to the left. Mules are used for lead positions because they follow instructions better than horses.

1913 SCHEDULE:

Lv. Shaniko	CS No. 1	8:00 A.M.	Monday
Ar. Biggs	CS No. 1	11:25 A.M.	Monday

The Great Southern Railroad has just arrived in Friend, Oregon, the end of the forty-mile line, and has spotted the coach in front of the railroad station. GS No. 1 (4-4-0) heads for the turntable to prepare for the return trip to The Dalles. A connection will be made in The Dalles with the Union Pacific for passengers, express and the U.S. Mail, Portland bound.

"The Presidents Special," pulled by coal burning engine No. 1300 (4-6-0), passes an over the line inspection in about 1917. E. E. Calvin, president of the Union Pacific system from 1916 to 1918, is making one of his frequent checks of his railroad. Conductor George M. Wilson can be seen standing on the ground with his hands on his hips. It is believed this picture was taken somewhere in eastern Oregon.

1913 SCHEDULE:

Lv. The Dalles	Great Southern No. 1	8:00 A.M.	Monday
Ar. Friend, Oreg.	Great Southern No. 1	10:45 A.M.	Monday
Lv. Friend	Great Southern No. 2	1:00 P.M.	Monday
Ar. The Dalles	Great Southern No. 2	3:45 P.M.	Monday
Lv. The Dalles	OR&N No. 17 Oregon-Washington Limited	3:45 P.M.	Monday
Ar. Portland	OR&N No. 17 Oregon-Washington Limited	6:30 P.M.	Monday

The eastbound "Salt Lake Express" pulls out of Huron, Oregon in the Blue Mountains in 1921

FEBRUARY 1921 SCHEDULE:

Lv. Portland	UP No. 24 Salt Lake Express	11:00 P.M.	Sunday
Ar. Huron, Oreg.	UP No. 24 Salt Lake Express	9:09 A.M.	Monday
Ar. Salt Lake City	UP No. 24 Salt Lake Express	8:15 A.M.	Tuesday

UP No. 18, "The Portland Limited," in 1926 awaits the conductor's "highball" before departure. The train is pulled by a Pacific-type locomotive No. 3227 (4-6-2). Note the automatic train control located in front of the lead pony truck. This highly sensitive instrument is automatically activated as the train passes over a problem undetected by the engineer such as might occur on excessively foggy nights. Note also the smoke deflector (the wire net above the stack). This was used to divert smoke away from the cab.

"The Portland Limited" in the Columbia River Gorge with Horsetail Falls to the right

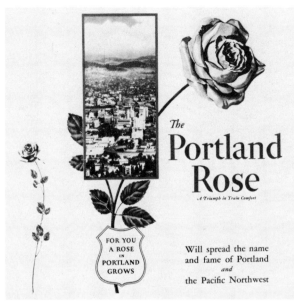

The "Portland Rose" — a triumph in train comfort. The citizens of Portland were delighted to have a train named after their beautiful city. This train name was in use from 1931 to 1950.

1932 SCHEDULE:

Lv. Portland	UP No. 18 Portland Rose	9:35 P.M.	Sunday
Ar. Chicago	UP No. 18 Portland Rose	8:45 A.M.	Wednesday

Dining Car Meals that Appeal

IT doesn't matter how fine the train equipment may be—if the dining car service isn't top-notch the trip is a failure as far as the passenger is concerned. Beautiful dining cars, skilful chefs and deft service are important parts of UNION PACIFIC train service.

They say—

"To start with, you have furnished excellent cooks, food, and equipment. Your steward, Mr........has a fine and courteous personality, and has the dining car crew thoroughly trained in every respect."

Mr. F. H. F ....
San Francisco, Calif.

They say—

"For the second time I've had the pleasure of being a passenger on your 'Columbine' train out of Denver, and it gives me the greatest pleasure to tell you that the excellence of the service and the beauty of the train is, I believe, unsurpassed on any road."

Mrs. W. E. K ....
San Diego, Calif.

Club Observation Cars

LOUNGE cars that are probably the finest examples of modern decoration, arrangement and furnishings—soft carpets, attractive upholstery, oil paintings on the walls, etched-glass partitions—altogether, an ideal harmony of color and comfort.

This new UP streamliner, a three-car train was on display in Portland in March 1934 and was the first train of its kind ever seen in the West. The *Oregonian* describes the visit: "This novel train consists of three cars for a total length of 204 feet of aluminum alloy painted a canary yellow and trimmed in brown."

On June 6, 1935 the "Streamliner City of Portland," a seven-car train commenced "sailings" from Portland to Chicago every six days. As there was only one train in the line, this was the best service the Union Pacific could offer. The service was discontinued on July 26, 1935. This operation was renewed February 6, 1936 to March 27, 1939 when it was replaced by an eleven-car train running six "sailings" a month with the same schedule. In 1947 the train began daily service.

UP Extra No. 3950 "Main Line Freight" in about 1945 pulled by a Challenger-type locomotive (4-6-6-4). "Bread and Butter Express" is a railroad man's classification of this type of train. The white flags indicate that this train is running extra — not governed by the timetable.

The westbound "Idahoan" arrives in Hood River on a clear, wintery day in 1947. Notice the cardboard boxes stacked on the handcar *(right)* which contain live baby chickens being shipped to Portland. The spout close to the track *(center)* furnishes water for the remaining steam engines. Also notice the 1929 Model A Ford Tudor.

1951 SCHEDULE:

Lv. Omaha, Nebraska	UP No. 11 The Idahoan	9:45 P.M.	Sunday
Ar. Hood River	UP No. 11 The Idahoan	1:50 P.M.	Tuesday
Ar. Portland	UP No. 11 The Idahoan	3:30 P.M.	Tuesday

UP No. 12, the "Idahoan," was first shown in the public timetable in 1947, the same year the "City of Portland" started daily service. It continued operating until November 1954 when only the "City of Portland" was left. This photo shows the "Idahoan" passing through The Dalles in about 1951. The UP telegraph operator is holding an "order hoop" with train orders for the conductor and engineer. These orders are written on thin tissue and are tied to a string at the top of the hoop. They can be removed easily by train crew members as the train passes through without stopping. Note the Sperry Rail Detector DC-2 on the far track. It is often called an "x-ray on wheels" because it is used to detect internal fissures that develop in the rails, as they are invisible to track inspectors and have frequently caused train derailments. The Sperry detector cars check for these defects by running over the rail while an instrument inside the car records imperfections by electrical impulses on a chart. When it locates an imperfection it will spray white paint on the rail at the defective spot.

1951 SCHEDULE:

Lv. Portland	UP No. 12 The Idahoan	8:10 A.M.	Sunday
Ar. The Dalles	UP No. 12 The Idahoan	10:15 A.M.	Sunday
Ar. Omaha, Nebraska	UP No. 12 The Idahoan	7:00 A.M.	Tuesday

UP No. 1, "The Mail Express Train," leaving
Baker, Oregon in 1952.

1952 SCHEDULE:

Lv. Portland	UP No. 26 The Mail Express	10:10 P.M.	Sunday
Ar. Baker	UP No. 26 The Mail Express	8:45 A.M.	Monday
Ar. Pocatello, Idaho	UP No. 26 The Mail Express	9:15 P.M.	Monday

The "Domeliner — City of Portland" in 1955 seen passing under the legendary "Bridge of the Gods" that crosses the Columbia
River near the city of Cascade Locks. The "Domeliner" was shown in the public timetable from 1955 to 1969.

Inside one of the domecars

1955 SCHEDULE:

Lv. Portland	UP No. 106 Domeliner — City of Portland	5:30 P.M.	Sunday
Ar. Chicago	UP No. 106 Domeliner — City of Portland	11:20 A.M.	Tuesday

UNION PACIFIC SYSTEM. 3ɪ

PRINCIPAL OFFICES:—Railroad Building, Omaha, Nebraska ; No. 44 Equitable Building, Boston, Mass.
Portland Office, Worcester Block, Corner Third and Oak Sts., Room 40.

EXECUTIVE DEPARTMENT.

SIDNEY DILLON, President, New York.
S. H. H. CLARK, General Manager, Omaha.
E. DICKINSON, Ass't Gen'l Manager, Omaha.
G. M. LANE, 2d Vice President, Boston.
T. L. KIMBALL, 3d Vice-President, Omaha.
OLIVER W. MINK, Comptroller, Boston.
Jas. G. HARRIS, Treasurer, Boston.
F. D. BROWN, Local Treasurer, Omaha.
ALEX. MILLAR, Secretary, Boston.

ACCOUNTING DEPARTMENT.

ERASTUS YOUNG, Auditor, Omaha.
F. W. HILLS, Asst. Auditor, Omaha.
RICHARD ANDERSON, Auditor of Disbursements, Omaha.
A. S. VAN KURAN, Freight Auditor, Omaha.
W. S. WING, Auditor Passenger Accounts, Omaha.
B. H. CALEF, General Traveling Auditor.

TRAFFIC DEPARTMENT.

C. S. MELLEN, General Traffic Manager, Omaha.

J. A. MUNROE, Gen. Freight Agent, Omaha.
B. CAMPBELL. G. W. F. A., Portland.
E. L. LOMAX, Genl. Pass. and Ticket Agent, Omaha.
J. W. SCOTT, Asst. Gen. Pass. Agt., Omaha.
W. H. HURLBURT, Ass't Gen. Pass. Agt., Portland, Or.
A. TRAYNOR, Genl. Baggage Agent, Council Bluffs, Ia.

OPERATING DEPARTMENT.

E. McNEILL, General Supt. Pacific Div., Portland.
EDWARD COOKINGHAM, Supt. Oregon Division.
WILL H. HOLCOMB, Supt. Wash. Div., Walla Walla, Wash.
E. BUCKINGHAM, Supt. Car Service, Omaha.
J. W. GRIFFETHS, Gen. Purchasing Agt., Omaha.
L. H KORTY, Supt. of Telegraph, Omaha.

LAW DEPARTMENT.

JOHN F. DILLON, General Counsel, New York,
JOHN M. THURSTON, General Solicitor, Omaha, Neb.
W. W. COTTON, General Attorney, Portland, Or.

EASTWARD.		Miles f'm Portland	Between Portland and Huntington Pacific time. June 1, 1891.	WESTWARD.	
Fast Mail. Daily.	Atlantic Exp.			Pacific Exp.	Fast Mail. Daily.
8 45P.M	8 00AM	0	Lv...**Portland**...Ar	9 45P.M	9 00AM
8 55AM	8 10AM	3	...East Portland..	9 35P.M	8 50AM
9 15P.M	8 30AM	10	......Clarnie......	9 15P.M	8 30AM
9 29P.M	8 45AM	15	......Fairview.....	8 55P.M	8 18AM
9 34P.M	8 53AM	18	...Troutdale.....	8 44P.M	8 08AM
9 54P.M	9 11AM	25	...Rooster Rock...	8 25P.M	7 50AM
9 56P.M	9 14AM	...	...Latourelle....	8 16P.M	7 41AM
10 04P.M	9 24AM	28	....Bridal Veil..	8 13P.M	7 38AM
10 14P.M	9 35AM	32	.Multnomah Falls..	8 03P.M	7 28AM
10 17P.M	9 40AM	33	......Oneonta...	7 58P.M	7 23AM
10 29P.M	9 50AM	37	......Dodson's	7 48P.M	7 12AM
10 40P.M	10 03AM	41	......Bonneville.....	7 35P.M	7 00AM
10 50P.M	10 15AM	45	...Cascade Locks..	7 25P.M	6 50AM
11 09P.M	10 35AM	52	......Wyeth	7 05P.M	6 34AM
11 24P.M	10 52AM	58	......Viento	6 50P.M	6 14AM
11 45P.M	11 14AM	66	....Hood River ...	6 30P.M	5 54AM
12 01AM	11 30AM	72	......Mosier......	6 13P.M	5 35AM
12 18AM	11 50AM	79	......Rowena....	5 52P.M	5 15AM
1 05AM	12 35P.M	88	.¶Dalles......	5 30P.M	4 50AM
1 25AM	12 50P.M	96	......Summit......	4 56P.M	4 12AM
1 40AM	1 05P.M	101	....Celilo......	4 42P.M	3 58AM
1 50AM	1 15P.M	104	....Des Chutes...	4 35P.M	3 47AM
2 00AM	1 25P.M	108	......Biggs........	4 25P.M	3 40AM
2 09AM	1 34P.M	111	......Grants	4 18P.M	3 30AM
2 25AM	1 50P.M	118	.....John Days.....	4 00P.M	3 14AM
2 37AM	2 05P.M	123	...Squally Hook....	3 47P.M	3 00AM
2 50AM	2 15AM	127	......Quinns	3 37P.M	2 50AM
3 05AM	2 35P.M	...	...... Blalocks	3 20P.M	2 36AM
3 25AM	3 00P.M	142	......**Arlington.** ..	3 00P.M	2 18AM
3 47AM	3 22P.M	151	.... Willows.....	2 40P.M	2 01AM
3 52AM	3 28P.M	152	...**Willows Junc**...	2 34P.M	1 58AM
4 17AM	3 52P.M	162	...Castle Rock...	2 18P.M	1 40AM
4 37AM	4 08P.M	170	.....Coyote.....	2 04P.M	1 23AM
5 00AM	4 27P.M	180	......Stokes.......	1 47P.M	1 05AM
5 30AM	4 50P.M	187	...**Umatilla Ju**...	1 35P.M	12 50AM
5 45AM	5 05P.M	193	...Maxwell.....	1 15P.M	12 22AM
6 05AM	5 25P.M	202	.... Fosters......	12 58P.M	12 05AM
6 15AM	5 32P.M	205	......Echo	12 52P.M	11 58P.M
6 30AM	5 45P.M	212	......Nolin.......	12 40P.M	11 45P.M
6 37AM	5 50P.M	215	......Yoakum.....	12 35P.M	11 40P.M
6 53AM	6 10P.M	223	.... Barnhart ...	12 20P.M	11 25P.M
7 10AM	6 30P.M	231	Ar) **Pendleton** (Lv	12 05P.M	11 10P.M
7 30AM	6 52P.M		Lv) (Ar	11 48AM	10 50P.M
7 33AM	6 55P.M	232	...**Pendleton Jun**...	11 48AM	10 50P.M
......	7 03P.M	235	......Mission	11 40AM	......
7 55AM	7 18P.M	242	....Cayuse	11 25AM	10 28P.M
8 20AM	7 38P.M	252	....Gibbon	11 00AM	10 08P.M
8 55AM	8 10P.M	263	......Wilbur	10 43AM	9 49P.M
8 57AM	8 12P.M	263	...North Fork ...	10 40AM	9 47P.M
9 26AM	8 30P.M	272	.....Huron......	10 20AM	9 28P.M
10 00AM	9 05P.M	280	.....Meacham.....	10 00AM	9 05P.M

EAST.		Mls f'm Portld	Pacific time—1 hour slower than Mountain time.	WEST.	
Fast Mail Daily.	Atl'ntc Exp.			Pacific Exp.	Fast Mail Daily.
10 20AM	9 30P.M	286	......Kamela......	9 40AM	8 45P.M
10 45AM	10 00P.M	297	......Hilgard......	8 45AM	7 55P.M
11 15AM	10 35P.M	305	.....La Grande.....	8 25AM	7 35P.M
11 35AM	11 00P.M	318	......Union.......	7 55AM	7 05P.M
12 15P.M	11 40P.M	327	....Telocaset	7 25AM	6 35P.M
12 37P.M	12 05AM	337	..North Powder...	7 00AM	6 10P.M
12 55P.M	12 25AM	347	.....Haines.....	6 40AM	5 53P.M
1 17P.M	12 50AM	357	...Baker City...	6 20AM	5 35P.M
1 35P.M	1 05AM	363	......Norton	6 05AM	5 17P.M
1 50P.M	1 30AM	367	......Encina	5 55AM	5 07P.M
1 55P.M	1 35AM	369	..Pleasant Valley ..	5 45AM	4 58P.M
2 17P.M	1 52AM	377	......Unity......	5 15AM	4 31P.M
2 35P.M	2 10AM	384	.....Durkee.....	4 55AM	4 10P.M
2 52P.M	2 25AM	392	.....Weatherby ..	4 35AM	3 47P.M
3 20P.M	3 00AM	404	Ar) .**Huntington**. (Lv	4 10AM	3 20P.M
4 30P.M	4 10AM	404	Lv) (Ar	......	......
Mo		**time**	**untain** e one hour faster th	**an Pac**	**ific**
5 26P.M	5 12AM	427	......Weiser......	3 26P.M	4 09AM
6 01P.M	5 40AM	440	......Payette	3 02P.M	3 43AM
6 10P.M	5 50AM	444	......Ontario	2 53P.M	3 35AM
7 25P.M	7 25AM	477	......Caldwell.....	2 28AM	1 50P.M
7 46P.M	7 45AM	496	.....**Nampa**	1 33P.M	2 10AM
9 50P.M	9 40AM	541	...Mountain Home..	11 45AM	12 20AM
11 10P.M	10 50AM	570	..Glenn's Ferry ..	10 40AM	10 55P.M
1 23AM	12 50P.M	622	.....**Shoshone**.....	8 44AM	8 51P.M
3 20AM	2 42P.M	...	...Minidoka...	7 05AM	7 03P.M
4 44AM	3 59P.M	704	...American Falls ..	5 58AM	5 50P.M
5 45AM	4 55P.M	730	Ar) **Pocatello** (Lv	5 10AM	4 55P.M
6 10AM	5 25P.M		Lv) (Ar	4 45AM	4 25P.M
		753	...McCauluon	......	......
8 55AM	8 05P.M	798	...Soda Springs ...	2 35AM	2 00P.M
10 40AM	11 00P.M	860	......Cokeville....	12 33AM	11 40AM
3 10P.M	2 30AM	944	......**Granger**	9 30P.M	8 20AM
4 10P.M	3 30AM	...	...Green River....	8 30P.M	7 10AM
9 45P.M	10 10AM		......Rawlins.....	3 10P.M	12 40AM
2 45AM	4 00P.M	1247	....**Laramie**	10 05AM	6 50P.M
5 10AM	6 50P.M	1304	Ar ..**Cheyenne**.. Lv	7 20AM	3 40P.M
5 30AM	7 ;5P.M	1304	Lv ..**Cheyenne**.. Ar	7 00AM	3 00P.M
9 25AM	12 10AM	1449	....**Julesburg**....	1 25AM	8 50AM
	Ce		**ntral t**ime 2 hours faster than	**Pacific**	
12 35P.M	4 15AM	...	...North Platte....	10 45P.M	6 05AM
3 08P.M	7 43AM	1625	......**Kearney**....	8 55P.M	3 20AM
4 20P.M	9 35AM	1666	..**Grand Island**...	7 45P.M	1 55AM
6 15P.M	11 45AM	1728	......**Columbus**.....	5 38P.M	11 20P.M
7 33P.M	1 25AM	1773	.....**Fremont**.....	4 24P.M	9 30P.M
......	......	1785	......**Valley**......	......	......
9 05P.M	3 30P.M	1820	......**Omaha**	2 50P.M	7 30P.M
9 30P.M	3 50P.M	1823	..**Council Bluffs**...	2 30P.M	7 00P.M
......	......	2310	Ar ..**Chicago** ...Lv	......	......
5 25AM	7 10P.M	1304	Lv...**Cheyenne** ..Ar	4 15AM	2 10P.M

The Pride of the Union Pacific: UP No. 9 (4-4-0) *(left)*, a steamer built by Rogers Locomotive Works in 1865 and rebuilt by the UP in 1882. UP train M-10,000 *(right)* "Streamliner City of Salina" was built in 1934.

THE GREAT NORTHERN RAILWAY

JAMES JEROME HILL, The Empire Builder, in building the Great Northern Railway (GN) was a very farsighted and astute businessman. He saw the tremendous possibilities of trade with the Orient. The Chinese who came to California in the 1850s made money and acquired expensive tastes in keeping with their incomes. They learned to eat the bread of the white man and liked it so well that they began shipping flour to their relatives in China. From this developed a complete change in what our country supplied and sold to the Orient. Flour never has and perhaps never will supplant rice as the great diet staple of the Orient but with their countless millions of population, even its moderate use as a necessity has created a tremendous growth and movement of this traffic.

As the movement of flour to the Orient increased, the silk from the Orient to the United States became a highly important commodity. Jim Hill with the aid of his own shipping lines built a very prosperous and successful freight business. His interest in the Orient resulted in the naming of his choice transcontinental train, the "Oriental Limited."

The Great Northern Flyer

The "Great Northern Flyer" was the outstanding train from 1899 to December 1905. During this period the GN advertised in its public timetables its "Route of the Pacific Fast Mail." GN was now handling transcontinental U.S. Government Mail over its tracks and in addition had secured a close working contract with Nippon Yusen Kaisha (a Japan Mail steamship line, sometimes called NYK) who had contracts to carry Japanese and Chinese mails. NYK service covered not only the entensive shoreline of Japan and China but extended north to Vladivostock, Siberia; south to Adelaide, Australia and west to Bombay, India.

1899 TO DECEMBER 1905 SCHEDULE:

Lv. Portland	OR&N No. 4 Spokane Flyer	6:00 P.M.	Sunday
Ar. Spokane, Wash.	OR&N No. 4 Spokane Flyer	9:15 A.M.	Monday
Lv. Spokane	GN No. 4 Great Northern Flyer	9:40 A.M.	Monday
Ar. St. Paul	GN No. 4 Great Northern Flyer	2:30 P.M.	Thursday

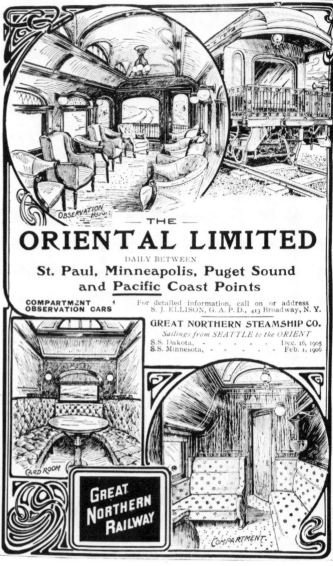

The Oriental Limited

In December 1905 the Great Northern started operating its new deluxe "Oriental Limited" still using the OR&N tracks from Portland to Spokane. On March 19, 1908 the first train moved over the North Bank Line, a railroad built by the Hill interests along the north side of the Columbia River. Jim Hill had secured control of the Chicago Burlington & Quincy Railroad (CB&Q) east of St. Paul and now had his own service Portland to Chicago over all of his own lines. Today this is The Burlington Northern.

1913 SCHEDULE:

Lv. Portland	SPS-GN-CB&Q No. 2 Oriental Limited	7:00 P.M.	Sunday
Ar. Chicago	SPS-GN-CB&Q No. 2 Oriental Limited	9:10 P.M.	Wednesday

320-Acre Free Homesteads for the Land-Hungry, and How To Get One.

160-Acre Homesteads, State School Lands and Indemnity School Lands. Desert Land Act and Timber and Stone Land Act Explained. A Few Facts About These Lands.

SYNOPSIS OF UNITED STATES HOMESTEAD LAWS

STOP and think what it would mean to you—your wife—your children—if you were absolutely independent. Suppose, after paying about $25.00 for legal papers, you could get a piece of this old earth's crust, half a mile long and a mile wide, just by living on the property for five years and cultivating the land. Then suppose you could raise flax, wheat and alfalfa. Flax (disinfect the seed before planting) will yield a good crop, which will civilize your land and bring a good cash profit. Horses, cattle, cows, hogs, sheep, goats, poultry and bees all thrive on alfalfa. You could also raise hay and other forage crops. This means pure milk, cheese, honey, bread and butter, wool, mohair, mutton and roast beef.

Wheat and your other surplus crops can be sold at a good profit. Nothing to buy except clothes, coffee, sugar and spices. If this prospect is attractive, read the rest.

Securing Your 320-Acre Homestead

Assuming that you are eligible, you would now take a delightful trip to Oregon, stopping at the federal land office nearest to your destination which *has jurisdiction or governs that Land District.*

Township plats, costing from $1 to $4, depending upon the information shown, can be bought from the Federal Land Officer. From this plat you can easily see what land is vacant and therefore subject to Homestead entry. Here you can also obtain the necessary legal blanks, which you must fill out and file, *after* you have examined your prospective homesteads, if you want this land.

Homestead applications can be filed at the land office which governs that Land District. Applications may also be filed before the following persons, in the county in which the land lies, *only after you have personally examined the land*—a register or receiver, a United States court or land commissioner, a judge in a court of record, a clerk in a court of record. You may also file before any officer of the classes named, who resides in the Land District, even if he resides outside the county, *provided he is the nearest and most accessible officer.* County clerks, U. S. commissioners or officers other than *the United States Land Commissioner,* who has jurisdiction over the land district where your filing is made, have no authority to *allow* any filings, being simply authorized to administer the oath.

The filing fees will cost you not more than $10.00. You will pay extra $1.50 for each forty-acre tract and other small fees required by the Homestead Law, amounting to about $25.00.

Within six months you must move on this land, establish a permanent home and legal residence. From that time you must cultivate your land every year and live on it for five years. (Leave of absence for short periods may, however, be obtained by application to the Land Office.) At least one-eighth of the land must be cultivated beginning with the second year of the entry, and at least one-quarter, each year, for the next three years. No specified amount of improvements, other than cultivation, are required, except that there must be enough improvements made to show good faith.

After residing on this land and cultivating it annually for five years, you must go to the Land Office and prove by at least two reliable witnesses, that you have cultivated and lived on the land as required, honestly and in good faith, for five years. Your final proofs, affidavits, etc., will be forwarded to the General Land Office, Washington, D. C., from whom you obtain a patent and a clear title to your land.

Great Northern advertisements of 1911 telling of free homestead lands for settlers coming into this vast agricultural area. The GN was just one of the western railroads that advertised and encouraged this type of traffic.

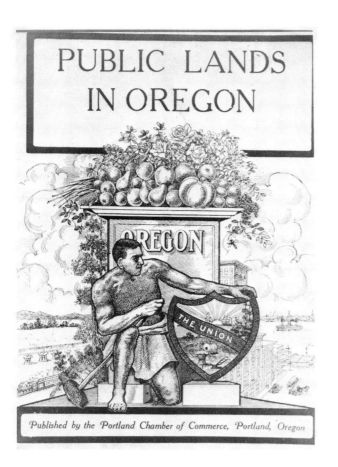

Three famous locomotives representing three different periods in railroad history line up in front of the North Bank Station, Portland, 1924. The trains are *(left to right):* 1) Great Northern Railway No. 2505 (4-8-2), the locomotive which pulled the "Oriental Limited" at the time; 2) GN No. 1, "The William Crooks" (4-4-0), locomotive of the 1860s. Behind this train is Pullman car No. 9, a replica of the first sleeping car; 3) "The Oregon Pony" (0-4-0), the first steam locomotive built in the Pacific Northwest. The three men standing on the ground are *(left to right):* W. S. Rotart, brakeman; W. D. McMillan, conductor; E. F. "Dad" Evans, station master; and Michael Maloney, all long-time employees of the Great Northern Railway.

The William Crooks

Great Northern engine No. 1, the "William Crooks" (4-4-0), arrived in St. Paul in 1861 on a Mississippi River steamboat. The little engine chugged its way from St. Paul on its initial passenger run to the village of St. Anthony, now known as Minneapolis, signaling the completion of the first ten miles of railroad in Minnesota. The railroad was the St. Paul & Pacific, Great Northern's original predecessor line. Locomotive No. 1 was named after the railroad's chief engineer, Col. William Crooks.

No. 9, a replica of the first sleeping car built by George Pullman, along with a dressed up cast to make the scene more real

George Pullman's First Sleeping Car

Pullman Car No. 9 was George Pullman's first sleeping car and made its first trip September 1, 1859 in Bloomington, Illinois on the Chicago & Alton Railroad. From the first trip it was related, "There was no crowd and the car, lighted by candles, moved away in solitary grandeur, if such it might be called. It was requested the passengers take their boots off before getting into the berths. The one passenger who removed his boots without compulsion was George Mortimer Pullman, the builder of the car. True, there were no sheets to soil, but boots in conjunction with a curtained bed of mattress and blanket did not form a perfect blending. This journey was the first on which an attempt was made to operate a car suitable for both night and day occupancy. It was the humble beginning of the Pullman Company."

The "Empire Builder," the top transcontinental train of the day, began operating from Portland to Chicago in 1929. The Great Northern System is known as "The Route of the Empire Builder." It pays tribute to the memory of James Jerome Hill and traverses the large territory to which Hill devoted his life.

1932–42 SCHEDULE:

Lv. Portland	SPS-GN-CB&Q No. 2 Empire Builder	9:30 P.M.	Sunday
Ar. Chicago	SPS-GN-CB&Q No. 2 Empire Builder	8:45 A.M.	Wednesday

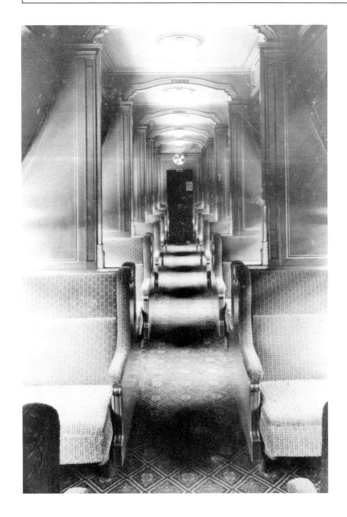

An inside view of a twelve-section, one drawing room Pullman car taken during the day hours. The drawing room is located at the extreme end of the aisle. Each section has both seats facing each other for lounging during the day, and at night offers an upper and lower berth for sleeping. Plumbing facilities are at each end of the car. A drawing room provides complete seclusion for an individual or family with a separate lavatory. Note the electric fan at the far end of the car. These were very important before air conditioning was introduced.

Oregon Historical Society Photo

Right, the "Empire Builder" in 1929 with berths ready for night use. Each section has a lower and upper berth, six feet long and forty-one inches wide. Note the safety ladder used for climbing into the upper berth.

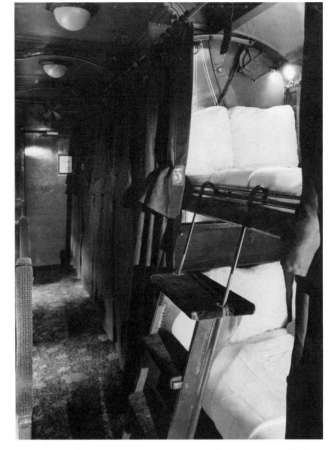

Below, a Pullman car upper berth was always a source of joke material for comedians because of the problem of climbing into the upper berth and the difficulty of removing your clothes. Note the hammock-like structure used for holding your belongings at night. Jokesters kidded about people climbing into the hammock supposedly believing this was the place to sleep. Note the electric bell available for calling the porter during the night.

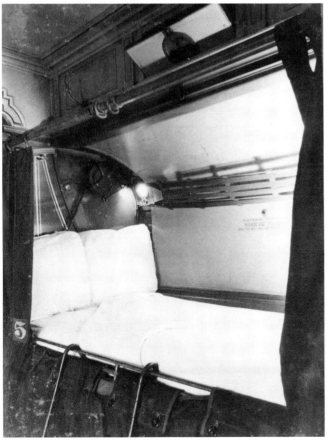

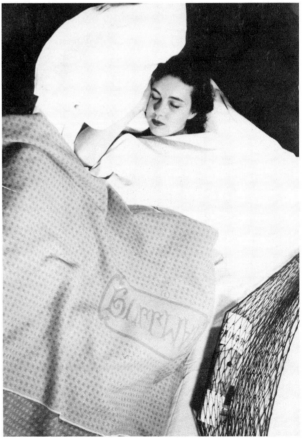

GN No. 459, the "Seattle Train," ready to leave Portland in 1935 pulled by engine No. 1028 (4-6-0 Baldwin). The Broadway Bridge crossing the Willamette River can be seen in the background.

1935 SCHEDULE:

Lv. Portland	SPS-NP-CB&Q No. 2 North Coast Limited	9:30 P.M.	Sunday
Ar. Chicago	SPS-NP-CB&Q No. 2 North Coast Limited	8:50 A.M.	Wednesday

1935 SCHEDULE:

Lv. Portland	GN No. 459 Seattle Train	4:20 P.M.	Monday
Ar. Seattle	GN No. 459 Seattle Train	9:20 P.M.	Monday

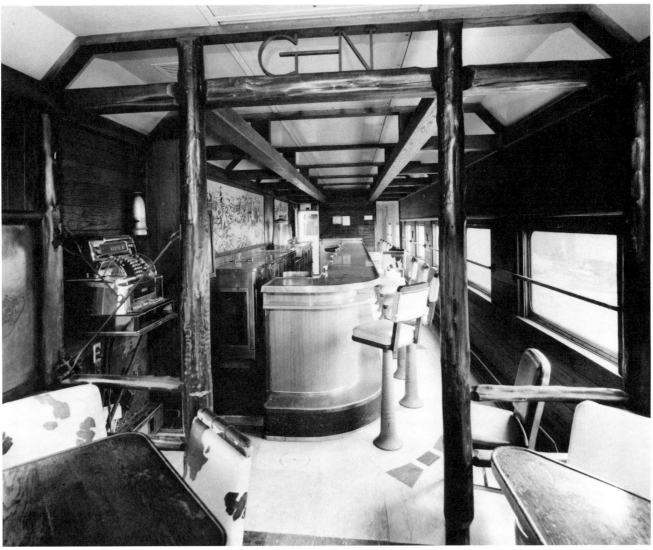

The new streamlined "Empire Builder" began running from Portland to Chicago in 1947. Amtrak took over in 1971.

1947–71 Schedule:

Lv. Portland	SPS-GN-CB&Q No. 2 Empire Builder	3:00 P.M.	Sunday
Ar. Chicago	SPS-GN-CB&Q No. 2 Empire Builder	2:00 P.M.	Tuesday

The "Fort Stevens Workhorse" in 1908, pulled by Astoria & Columbia River Railroad No. 3 (4-4-0), stops at Ft. Stevens at the mouth of the Columbia River. This mixed train handled both freight and passenger business between Astoria and Ft. Stevens. It also did the switching at Astoria and Warrentown including making up trains, turning equipment and other miscellaneous yard duties. The train crew is *(left to right):* Harry Beckett, conductor; Clarence Gaffney, brakeman; Harry Ellers, messenger; Bill Yested, brakeman; Joe Fake, engineer; and Tom Krager, fireman. Note the plank road.

1908 SCHEDULE:

Lv. Portland	ACR No. 3 Beach Special	9:20 A.M.	Monday
Ar. Astoria	ACR No. 3 Beach Special	12:10 P.M.	Monday
Lv. Astoria	ACR No. 23 Fort Stevens Workhorse	12:20 P.M.	Monday
Ar. Fort Stevens	ACR No. 23 Fort Stevens Workhorse	12:55 P.M.	Monday

ACR No. 2, "The Beach Special," in 1910 returning from the Coast, is shown stopped at Scappoose, Oregon, pulled by engine No. 55 (4-4-0).

1910 SCHEDULE:

Lv. Holladay (Seaside)	ACR No. 2 Beach Special	7:20 A.M.	Monday
Ar. Scappoose	ACR No. 2 Beach Special	11:23 A.M.	Monday
Ar. Portland	ACR No. 2 Beach Special	12:05 P.M.	Monday

162

Operating the Floating
PALACES OF THE PACIFIC
S. S. "GREAT NORTHERN" — S. S. "NORTHERN PACIFIC"
BETWEEN
SAN FRANCISCO and PORTLAND, via ASTORIA

SAILING SCHEDULE
(Subject to change without notice)

NORTHBOUND	SOUTHBOUND
Every Tuesday, Thursday and Saturday	Every Tuesday, Thursday and Saturday
Lv San Francisco (G.N.P.S.S.Co.) 10.30 am	Lv Portland - (S.P.&S.Ry.) 9.30 am
Ar Flavel-Astoria " " 12.30 pm next day	Ar Flavel-Astoria " " 1.00 pm
Lv Flavel-Astoria (S.P.&S.Ry.) 1.00 pm	Lv Flavel-Astoria (G.N.P.S.S.Co.) 1.30 pm
Ar Portland - " " 4.25 pm	Ar San Francisco " " 3.30 pm next day

Flavel, Oregon, seven miles west of Astoria, showing the "high sheds" built to protect passengers from Oregon rains. A Great Northern Pacific Steamship has just docked and patrons are waiting for the "Steamer Express" to take them back to Portland.

The "Steamer Express," which in 1915 operated every Tuesday, Thursday and Saturday for connection with the S.S. *Great Northern* and the S.S. *Northern Pacific*, a three and one-half-hour trip from Flavel to Portland.

The Great Northern Pacific Steamship Company

When rail and ocean service for passengers traveling from Portland to San Francisco began in 1915 by James J. Hill, who controlled the Great Northern Pacific Steamship Company, the total cost was the same as rail fare from Portland to San Francisco on a SP rail line and in addition included a berth and meals while at sea. The trip took only three hours longer than SP's fastest train and included rail to Flavel and steamship to San Francisco. The two ships that traveled the route, the S.S. *Northern Pacific* and the S.S. *Great Northern*, were 509 feet long and carried 839 passengers. Service was started during the Panama-Pacific International Exposition held in San Francisco in 1915 and continued until 1917 when the two ships were commandeered by the U.S. Government for troopships during World War I. The S.S. *Northern Pacific* was sunk and the S.S. *Great Northern* was sold after the war to the Admiral Lines and renamed the S.S. *H.F. Alexander*.

Left, the eastbound "Inland Empire Express" in 1916 passing through a 2,369-foot tunnel at Cape Horn, Washington. The Columbian River can be seen in the background.

CITY OF PRINEVILLE RAILWAY

TIME TABLE NO. 4.

EFFECTIVE 12:01 A. M. SUNDAY, NOVEMBER 9, 1919

West Bound				STATIONS		East Bound		
Mixed No. 5	Motor No. 3	Motor No. 1				Motor No. 2	Motor No. 4	Mixed No. 6
P.M.	P.M.	A.M.				A.M.	P.M.	P.M.
6:20	5:30	5:15	Lv.	PRINEVILLE	Ar.	7:30	7:50	9:45
6:35	5:45	5:30	Lv.	WILTON	Ar.	7:15	7:35	9:30
7:05	6:15	6:05	Lv.	O'NEIL	Ar.	6:50	7:05	9:00
7:20	6:30	6:20	Ar.	PRINEVILLE JUNCTION	Lv.	6:35	6:50	8:45

Daily Freight service.

Connections at Prineville Junction with Oregon Trunk 102 and 105 and O. W. R. & N. 36. Do not wait for O. W. R. & N. 35

Stages for Post, Paulina, Suplee and Izee leave Prineville daily except Sunday. For Ochoco, Roberts, Barnes and Fife on Mondays, Wednesdays and Fridays.

American Railway Express.

Through tickets sold from all O. W. R. & N. and S. P. & S. points.
West bound trains have right of track.
At meeting point allow five minutes for variation of time.

The "City of Prineville Railway" connected with "The Bend Local" at Prineville Junction in 1932.

OT train "The Bend Local," in 1932. The Oregon Trunk Railroad crosses and recrosses the Deschutes River before reaching Bend, Oregon.

1932 SCHEDULE:

Lv. Portland	SPS No. 2 North Bank Limited	9:30 P.M.	Sunday
Ar. Wishram, Wash.	SPS No. 2 North Bank Limited	12:17 A.M.	Monday
Ar. Pasco, Wash.	SPS No. 2 North Bank Limited	3:05 A.M.	Monday
Ar. Spokane, Wash.	SPS No. 2 North Bank Limited	7:00 A.M.	Monday

Cars carried for the "Bend Local":

Lv. Wishram	OT No. 102 Bend Local	12:30 A.M.	Monday
Ar. Prineville Junction	OT No. 102 Bend Local	6:40 A.M.	Monday
Ar. Bend	OT No. 102 Bend Local	7:40 A.M.	Monday

(An immediate connection is made with the City of Prineville Railway for the eighteen-mile trip from Prineville Junction to Prineville.)

Cars carried for the "North Coast Limited":

Lv. Pasco	NP No. 2 North Coast Limited	3:22 A.M.	Monday
Ar. Chicago	NP No. 2 North Coast Limited	9:00 A.M.	Wednesday

Cars carried for the "Empire Builder":

Lv. Spokane	GN No. 2 Empire Builder	7:45 A.M.	Monday
Ar. Chicago	GN No. 2 Empire Builder	8:45 A.M.	Wednesday

"The Bend Local" arrives in Bend, Oregon in 1932 pulled by locomotive No. 600 (4-4-2 Baldwin) while the train crew has its picture taken. *Left to right:* Conductor Frank P. Allen; Engineer Tom Blake; Fireman "Pete" Peterson; Brakeman Jim Thomas; and others unknown.

OT No. 102, "The Bend Mixed Train" (called that because it handled both passenger and freight equipment), arriving in Bend pulled by SPS diesel No. 82.

1967 Schedule:

Lv. Portland	SPS No. 4 Spokane Local	9:45 P.M.	Monday
Ar. Wishram, Wash.	SPS No. 4 Spokane Local	11:46 P.M.	Monday
Lv. Wishram	OT No. 102 Bend Mixed Train	1:00 A.M.	Tuesday
Ar. Bend	OT No. 102 Bend Mixed Train	7:00 A.M.	Tuesday

THE OREGON ELECTRIC RAILWAY

THE OREGON ELECTRIC RAILWAY COMPANY (OE) was built by eastern capitalists as an electric line between Portland and Salem. Track crews started at both Portland and Salem ends. The last spike was driven at Tigardville (Tigard) November 20, 1907. *The Oregonian* carried the story: "No gilded spike was driven and there were no officials at the completion of the track laying."

The 49.7 miles of track were thrown open for passenger service on January 1, 1908. The Forest Grove branch, an additional nineteen miles, was completed and in operation by December, 1908.

In March, 1910 James Jerome Hill, The Empire Builder, purchased the line and continued building from Salem to Albany and Eugene. Also about the same time he secured ownership of the United Railways and tied the two lines together under one operation.

Hill had long dreamed of having his own rail service into the state of California and of sharing in the heavy movement of both passenger and freight business accruing in the Willamette Valley. The Southern Pacific up until this time practically ruled the West Coast area. The SP kept the fire hot and eventually blocked every avenue of entrance south of Eugene and Hill was forced to build through Central Oregon to reach his destination.

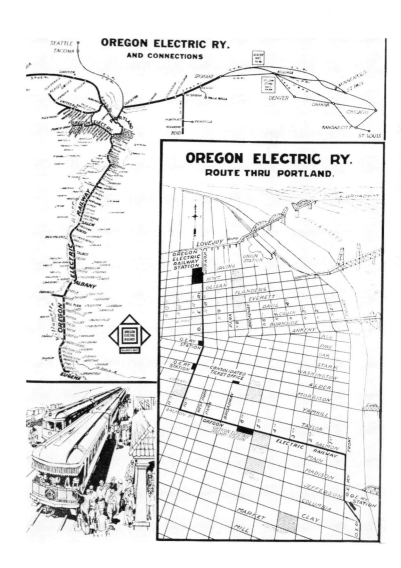

The building of the Oregon Electric Railway. This photo shows the crew laying ties and track as the line progresses toward Eugene. SPS No. 352 (Brooks 2-8-0) is a former GN engine loaned out to build the Oregon Electric Railway.

The first train to reach Hillsboro, Oregon, did so by way of the Forest Grove branch of the Oregon Electric Railway on September 15, 1908.

NOVEMBER 15, 1908 SCHEDULE:

Lv. Portland	OE No. 35 Forest Grove Passenger	10:25 A.M.	Monday
Ar. Hillsboro	OE No. 35 Forest Grove Passenger	11:30 A.M.	Monday
Ar. Forest Grove	OE No. 35 Forest Grove Passenger	11:45 A.M.	Monday

The Woodburn branch of the Oregon Electric Railway was finished on March 27, 1910 and carried the "Woodburn Local." This photo is of Extra Train No. 51, "Sunday Overflow," stopping at West Woodburn. On many Sundays and holidays it was necessary to operate extra trains to handle overflow crowds. The white flags indicate that the train was not covered by the timetable. Conductor Gus Bullard is standing on the ground at the head of the train.

MARCH 10, 1914 SCHEDULE:

Lv. Portland	OE No. 7 Eugene Local	10:40 A.M.	Monday
Ar. West Woodburn	OE No. 7 Eugene Local	12:22 P.M.	Monday
Lv. West Woodburn	OE No. 115 Woodburn Local	12:23 P.M.	Monday
Ar. Scollard	OE No. 115 Woodburn Local	12:25 P.M.	Monday
Ar. Woodburn	OE No. 115 Woodburn Local	12:31 P.M.	Monday

OE No. 51 approaching Scollard, the only intermediate stop for the three-mile trip to Woodburn

The "Rose City Limited" in 1912 at Garden Home en route to Portland. The track *(left)* is to Forest Grove. The orderboard is "red" which means the train must stop for passengers or train orders and cannot proceed until given a clearance by the operator inside the Garden Home Station.

JUNE 7, 1912 SCHEDULE:

Lv. Salem	OE No. 14 Rose City Limited	3:30 P.M.	Monday
Ar. Garden Home	OE No. 14 Rose City Limited	4:50 P.M.	Monday
Ar. Portland	OE No. 14 Rose City Limited	5:25 P.M.	Monday

Left, the "Rose City Limited" at Salem shortly before departure. The state capitol building can be seen in the background.

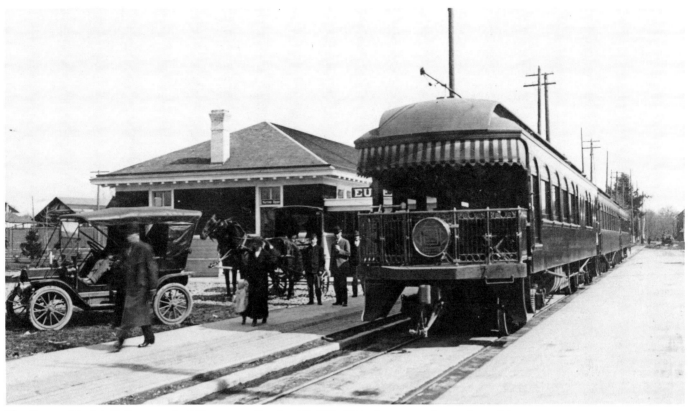

The Oregon Electric Railway reached Eugene on October 17, 1912. This photo was taken in front of the Eugene Station soon after an arrival from Portland. The auto shown is a 1909 or 1910 Buick.

Journal Photo

The Oregon Electric Railway arrives in Albany on its maiden trip July 4, 1912. Hundreds of people accorded an enthusiastic reception for the new train. The first official train from Portland brought over eight hundred businessmen and their families. The auto with the flag and the one directly in front of it are 1909 and 1910 Locomobiles, while the one to the left is a 1910 Ford Touring.

MARCH 10, 1914 SCHEDULE:

Lv. Salem	OE No. 9 Eugene Local	2:05 P.M.	Monday
Ar. Albany	OE No. 9 Eugene Local	5:35 P.M.	Monday
Ar. Eugene	OE No. 9 Eugene Local	7:05 P.M.	Monday

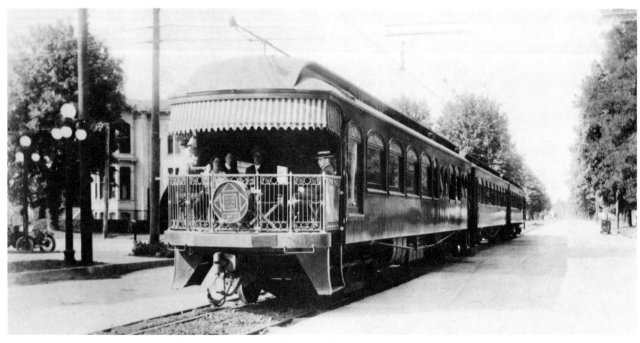

An Oregon Electric train passing through Albany en route to Portland in about 1918

The OE branch line to Corvallis was finished on March 22, 1913. Car No. 53 waits at Gray Station for the arrival of a Portland train and will handle Corvallis passengers to their destination.

July 4, 1928 Schedule:

Lv. Portland	OE No. 9 Eugene Local	2:05 P.M.	Monday
Ar. Gray	OE No. 9 Eugene Local	4:58 P.M.	Monday
Lv. Gray	OE No. 213 Corvallis Local	4:59 P.M.	Monday
Ar. Corvallis	OE No. 213 Corvallis Local	5:14 P.M.	Monday

Car No. 53 has arrived in Corvallis after making the five-mile run from the main line at Gray

The Oregon Electric line was opened to Salem on January 1, 1908. This photo shows an OE train stopping at Salem en route to Portland while the train crew has its picture taken. The two center people are *(left to right):* George Owen, brakeman; and William Henry Bretz, conductor. The rear car is "The Champoeg," a sixty-two-foot open end observation car. To ride in this car from Portland to Salem cost thirty-five cents plus the cost of a regular coach ticket. The building with a tower is the IOOF (International Order of Oddfellows) Building and was the first ticket office for the OE.

JUNE 19, 1922 SCHEDULE:

Lv. Portland	OE No. 5 Eugene Local	8:30 A.M.	Monday
Ar. Salem	OE No. 5 Eugene Local	10:15 A.M.	Monday
Ar. Eugene	OE No. 5 Eugene Local	12:25 P.M.	Monday

All of these engines are Oregon Electric "Work-horses" — two electric freight engines. SPS No. 51 was built in the Spokane Portland & Seattle Railway shops. It was sold to the Ft. Dodge Des Moines & Southern Railway at the time the line was converted to steam and diesel on July 10, 1945.

An eastbound electric freight train crossing the Willamette River over the high bridge at Wilsonville, headed toward Portland. Notice the ferry in the middle of the river.

An electric passenger train crosses the bridge at Wilsonville, heading westbound to Eugene

The United Railway (UR) during its construction days of 1910. This picture was taken somewhere along the twenty-seven-mile electric railroad.

SEPTEMBER 15, 1912 SCHEDULE:

Lv. Portland	UR No. 11	10:15 A.M.	Monday
Ar. Burlington	UR No. 11	11:05 A.M.	Monday
Ar. North Plains	UR No. 11	11:34 A.M.	Monday
Ar. Wilkesboro	UR No. 11	11:50 A.M.	Monday

(Oct 26, 1912)

PORTLAND'S INTERURBAN AND STREETCAR SERVICE

PORTLAND'S ELECTRIC INTERURBAN service to Oregon City, Gresham and Estacada along with its fine streetcar system starting from horse drawn vehicles to the fast, modern type of equipment, is a fascinating and well-documented story. (*Fares Please* by John Labbe is a delightful book of Portland's streetcar system.) The East Side Railway Company and later the Portland Railway Light & Power Company in 1893 built a sixteen-mile railroad between Portland and Oregon City — the first long distance electric railway system in America.

The company prospered for well over half a century as the surrounding country and Portland itself had a steady growth due in great part to the availability of this electrical transportation.

In 1913 *The London Times* reported that Portland would soon have the third most extensive electric railway system in America. It was a fine system, well-patronized and deserving of the highest commendation. But alas, progress brought the private automobile and fast trucks served by state and federal built freeways that shortened distances and reached beyond the electric train tracks. Business continued to drop until the company was forced to end its services.

Above, a 1913 advertisement

After the passenger business was discontinued the Southern Pacific and the Union Pacific bought up the interurban line and incorporated it into their own rail systems.

Below, a 1911 advertisement

PORTLAND-ESTACADA ELECTRIC TRAIN.

SEVEN DAILY TRAINS BETWEEN PORTLAND

AND

GRESHAM, ANDERSON, BORING, BARTON, EAGLE CREEK, CURRINSVILLE, ESTACADA AND CAZADERO

CARS EVERY 40 MINUTES BETWEEN PORTLAND AND OREGON CITY

FREIGHT TRAINS DAILY EXCEPT SUNDAY

MILK AND CREAM SHIPMENTS GIVEN PASSENGER TRAIN SERVICE

Ticket Office and Waiting Room, First and Alder Streets.   Freight Depot, East Water Street and Hawthorne Avenue

An advertisement for interurban train service, 1905

Portland's new open end vestibule cars — the very latest in 1900

Portland Traction Company No. 4007 in 1940 arrives in Gresham, Oregon, the end of the passenger line. A motorman is shown reversing the trolley in preparation for the return trip to Portland.

The East Side Railway Company name was later changed to the Portland Railway Light & Power Company. This photo shows a head-end car in 1905 receiving American Express Lading for delivery to Oregon City and way points. Note the Hawthorne Bridge towers in the extreme right.